Retreat
in the Real World

Loyola Press in partnership with Creighton University's Online Ministry

Retreat
in the Real World

Finding Intimacy
with God
Wherever You Are

A Self-Guided Ignatian Experience

Andy Alexander, SJ,
Maureen McCann Waldron,
and Larry Gillick, SJ

with black & white photography by Don Doll, SJ

LOYOLA PRESS.
A JESUIT MINISTRY
Chicago

LOYOLA PRESS.
A JESUIT MINISTRY

3441 N. Ashland Avenue
Chicago, Illinois 60657
(800) 621-1008
www.loyolapress.com

Imprimi Potest: G. Thomas Krettek, SJ, Provincial of the Wisconsin Province of the Society of Jesus

The "For the Journey" weekly resource was written by Larry Gillick, SJ
Cover design: Judine O'Shea
Interior design: Becca Gay
Black & white photography: Don Doll, SJ

The material in this book was developed for and originally appeared on Creighton University's Online Ministries Web site (http://onlineministries.creighton.edu/CollaborativeMinistry/cmo-retreat.html).

Library of Congress Cataloging-in-Publication Data

Alexander, Andy.
  Retreat in the real world : finding intimacy with God wherever you are : a self-guided Ignatian experience / Andy Alexander, Maureen McCann Waldron, and Larry Gillick.
    p. cm.
  ISBN-13: 978-0-8294-2913-8
  ISBN-10: 0-8294-2913-1
  1. Spiritual life--Catholic Church. 2. Spirituality--Catholic Church. 3. Ignatius, of Loyola, Saint, 1491-1556. I. Waldron, Maureen McCann. II. Gillick, Larry. III. Title.
  BX2350.3.A445 2009
  248.3--dc22
                              2009017859

Printed in the United States of America
12 13 14 15 Versa 10 9 8 7 6 5 4

Dedication

For Fred and Grace Alexander, for Jim Waldron,
and for Milly Jolly and Pat Walsh, SJ,
who have carried this ministry in prayer.

Contents

Introduction

The Creighton University Online Retreat, from which this book originates, began with requests from our faculty and staff, which went something like this: "We understand that those *Spiritual Exercises* are really central to the mission of this university. How can I get a copy to read?" We would explain to them that St. Ignatius's Exercises are a 450-year-old collection of guidelines and prayer experiences, which Ignatius wrote based on his own religious renewal for people who would guide other people in opening themselves to an experience of conversion. The book is full of directions and exercises, which he continually suggests should be adapted to the person making the retreat. Ignatius tells the director of the retreat—the one reading the book—that the person making the retreat should give thirty days, away from family and friends, to make the experience. He adds that some people can't give that kind of time to the Exercises, so they should be adapted for a longer time and should be made in the midst of their everyday, busy lives. Often faculty and staff would look sad and regret that there wasn't something more accessible for them, so they could experience what these Exercises were all about.

Since our Daily Reflections on our Online Ministries Web site had become so popular, we asked ourselves, "How would Ignatius want us to adapt his Exercises for today? Wouldn't he urge us to adapt them for busy people today, so that people could make them online, over thirty-four weeks, 24/7, from anywhere in the world?" We spent eight months adapting the movements of Ignatius's Exercises into the Online Retreat. The central goal of the retreat is to grow in spiritual freedom, specifically to be able to make choices more freely. Another goal of the retreat is to help a person become "a contemplative in action," finding "intimacy with God in the midst of action," so we decided to design the retreat so that a person making it this way would learn how to practice this very contemporary spirituality. The retreat would not require much time in formal prayer. What would be more central would be learning how to place the material of the retreat into the "background" of one's consciousness throughout each day and to let the material interact with the real events of ordinary life. That's where the fruit of this retreat would be found and how the grace would be given.

The retreat that evolved became thirty-four weekly guides, accompanied by a series of resources. The first resource was thirty-four photos by our dear friend and colleague, the gifted Jesuit photographer Don Doll, SJ. From among his thousands of powerful photographs we chose thirty-four to provide a visual experience of the grace being prayed for each week. We asked Fr. Larry Gillick, SJ, a mentor, colleague, and the director of our Center for Ignatian Spirituality, to write a reflective piece, called "For the Journey," to accompany each week.

We encourage people making the retreat to make the retreat with a spiritual guide, to do it with a group of friends, or to make it alone. In whatever way a person makes the retreat, we encourage people to use this book in conjuction with the online version. It can be found at the Creighton University Online Ministries Web site at http://onlineministries.creighton .edu/CollaborativeMinistry/cmo-retreat.html. Since this book does not include the Readings and Prayers of the online version, these resources may be found there. We especially encourage people to take part in the opportunity to share the graces of the retreat and to give feedback online at the end of the retreat experience. Thousands of people e-mail their experience of the graces they are receiving each week of the retreat. Anyone making the retreat can go to the sharing and read what others experience when they make the retreat. So, even if a person makes the retreat alone, the experience is one of making the retreat in the midst of a very large community.

It was Loyola Press's idea to offer the text of the Online Retreat in this book form. We are delighted that it expands the availability of this opportunity to be touched by the Exercises of Ignatius. There are many other adaptations of the Exercises available around the world. This adaptation allows a person to make the retreat with nothing else but this book and an open heart. It has the added advantage of allowing a person, with Internet access, to use the online version for additional resources and to experience the sharing part of the retreat. While making the retreat, one can make the photo for the week the photo on his or her computer desktop, as a reminder throughout that week of the graces being prayed for.

Consider making this retreat with someone else or gathering a group together to make the retreat. A group could meet weekly, or even monthly, to share the graces of the retreat. Some people make the retreat with a close friend or with other members of a group, e-mailing their sharing to one another every week. Please consider contributing your reflections to the sharing available on the Web site www.onlineministries .creighton.edu/CollaborativeMinistry/cmo-retreat.html.

We are grateful to St. Ignatius and all the Jesuits and lay colleagues who have taught us the power of the *Spiritual Exercises*. We thank all the people who have made the Online Retreat around the world and all who have supported us along the way. We are especially indebted to Creighton University for its generous support for our Online Ministries. Our office is very small, and we are deeply grateful for Carol Krajicek for her ongoing help and support.

Andy Alexander, SJ
Maureen McCann Waldron
Creighton University
Omaha, Nebraska

A Calendar to Make the Retreat with the Liturgical Year

The retreat may be started at any time of the year. However, if a person begins the retreat in mid-September, the retreat works with the liturgical year. This is accomplished by adding optional review weeks when necessary to adapt the retreat to the timing of Easter, which is a movable feast. These review weeks occur after Weeks 15, 17, and 21.

2009
Begin the retreat the week of September 13.
No review weeks are needed this year.
Ash Wednesday is February 17 and Easter Sunday is April 4, 2010.

2010
Begin the retreat the week of September 19.
Add review weeks after Week 15, Week 17, and Week 21.
Ash Wednesday is March 9 and Easter Sunday is April 24, 2011.

2011
Begin the retreat the week of September 18.
No review weeks are needed this year.
Ash Wednesday is February 22 and Easter Sunday is April 8, 2012.

2012
Begin the retreat the week of September 16.
Combine Weeks 20 and 21 into a single week.
Ash Wednesday is February 13 and Easter Sunday is March 31, 2013.

2013

Begin the retreat the week of September 15.

Use review weeks after Week 15 and Week 17.

Ash Wednesday is March 5 and Easter Sunday is April 20, 2014.

2014

Begin the retreat the week of September 14.

No review weeks are needed this year.

Ash Wednesday is February 18 and Easter Sunday is April 5, 2015.

2015

Begin the retreat the week of September 13.

Combine Weeks 20 and 21 into a single week.

Ash Wednesday is February 10 and Easter Sunday is March 27, 2016.

2016

Begin the retreat the week of September 18.

Use the review week after Week 15.

Ash Wednesday is March 1 and Easter Sunday is April 16, 2017.

2017

Begin the retreat the week of September 17.

Combine Weeks 20 and 21 into a single week.

Ash Wednesday is February 14 and Easter Sunday is April 1, 2018.

2018

Begin the retreat the week of September 16.

Use review weeks after Week 15 and Week 17.

Ash Wednesday is March 6 and Easter Sunday is April 21, 2019.

2019

Begin the retreat the week of September 15.

Use the review week after Week 15.

Ash Wednesday is February 26 and Easter Sunday is April 12, 2020.

How Do I Get Started Making the Retreat?

Each of the weeks of the retreat begins with a Guide page that lays out how to make that week of the retreat. The Guide page gives the theme of the week, particularly the grace to pray for that week. Following the weekly guide are the resources you can use with that week.

- **The Photo** This image helps us focus during the week.

- **Practical Helps** Additional help for beginning a particular week and shaping one's reflection during the week.

- **For the Journey** Fr. Larry Gillick, SJ, writes a simple reflection for the week as an aid to entering the week more deeply.

- **In These or Similar Words . . .** A help for praying with our own words, with an invitation to personalize your prayer.

- **Readings** Readings from Scripture or other sources that support the graces for that week.

Each week is different in the graces asked for and in the material reflected upon. And one week builds upon another. The growth is progressive and step-by-step.

The Retreat uses the movements of the Spiritual Exercises to help us grow in spiritual freedom and the ability to find intimacy with God in the midst of our everyday busy lives.

When should I start the retreat? The retreat can be started at any time. We offer the option of making the retreat with the liturgical year, by beginning in about the middle of September each year. This is especially wonderful for people in a family or for friends, or for groups of people in a parish, making the retreat together.

So, how do I do this? It's simple. Early in the week, read the Guide page and the other resources provided for each week. They will shape what you do during the upcoming week. Usually, the invitation is to let the grace you are praying for become a part of the background of your daily life. Asking for that grace in the morning, and staying conscious of that grace throughout the day, will allow that grace, that reflection, to interact with the events, conversations, meetings, and challenges of each day. And spending a few moments each night to express our gratitude for what we have received will begin to shape each very interactive week with God—my asking and opening my heart, and God being patient and generous with me.

Most of all, trust in God. God will not be outdone in generosity.

Prayer to Begin Each Day

Lord, I so wish to prepare well for this time.
I so want to make all of me ready and attentive and available to you.
Please help me clarify and purify my intentions.
I have so many contradictory desires.
My activity seems to be so full of busyness
and running after stuff that doesn't really seem to matter or last.
I know that if I give you my heart
whatever I do will follow my new heart.
May all that I am today,
all that I try to do today,
may all my encounters, reflections,
even the frustrations and failings
all place my life in your hands.

Lord, my life is in your hands.
Please, let this day give you praise.

You are the one
who put me together
    inside my mother's body,
and I praise you because of
the wonderful way
    you created me.

—Psalm 139

Let's Begin at the Beginning: Our Life Story

Guide: The Memories That Have Shaped Us

This is the first week of a thirty-four-week journey. We begin at the beginning—our story. Prayer is about our relationship with God. We will begin to grow in this relationship with God, in the midst of our everyday lives this week, by simply reflecting upon our own story. There may be times we will want to take a period of prayer to reflect upon our story this week. What is most important, however, is that we begin by letting this reflection become the *background* of our week.

Did you ever get a song in your head and realize that it was there for a long time, no matter what you were doing? This is like that. Throughout our day, each day this week, we will have in mind the *memories* that have shaped us.

Let this be the image: This week, let's go through the photo album of our life. Let's go back to our earliest memories. Let's let the Lord show us our lives. What pictures are there? With each part of my life, what scenes do I remember? Who is in those scenes? Some photos will be of happy times, some will be quite sad, others will be difficult to recollect at all. They all constitute our story and the journey that has brought us to where we begin this retreat.

Take it easy. Go slowly. Take a little bit each day. Being faithful to this exercise will help tremendously to prepare for the weeks ahead. Write down notes or memories or stories if you'd like.

End each day, before going to bed, with a few interior words of gratitude to the One who has accompanied me through my life, even to this day of presence with me.

Some Practical Help for Getting Started This Week

The first and most important point is to begin this journey with great hope and confidence. God is never outdone in generosity. So, if we make even a small change in our weekly pattern, that is a tremendous *opening* for God to work in us. One way to affirm this hope and confidence is to express it for just a brief instant, each morning, *at the same time each day*—as I'm finding my slippers, or as I'm brushing my teeth, or while I'm pouring that first cup of coffee—"I know you are with me today, Lord."

Each of us will have a different amount of time we will be able to give to this retreat each week. We recommend that if your time is limited, just read the guide. On another day that week, you may find you have time to return to reflect on another resource.

This week's guide offers us the opportunity to review our life stories through the *photo album* of our lives. Throughout these weeks, we'll make use of the practice, habit, exercise of letting a reflection or image be part of the *background* of our day. All of us are aware, from time to time, that there is stuff that occupies the *background* of our consciousness. The song that plays in our head is a common example. This retreat invites us to practice taking advantage of this facility our brain has. Rather than have that *space* filled *at random* with stuff that just comes and goes, we will *focus it more consciously*. While doing all the ordinary tasks we do in our everyday lives, we will be using that *background space* to give a distinctive *tone* to our week. This won't be a *distraction* to our work, or take any extra time away from our work, but it will eventually make a difference in how we experience our work. It just takes practice.

Concretely, for this week, we all know the outline of our story. This isn't *new* material. What is new is that I will consciously be aware that I am reviewing my life story this week. I can plan it fairly deliberately—as an example: Monday and Tuesday, I will be remembering the images of my childhood; Wednesday and Thursday, my teens and early adulthood; Friday and Saturday, the rest of my adult life. So, throughout Wednesday—as I'm finding my slippers, driving to work, walking to my first meeting, walking to the restroom, looking at that image on my monitor, walking to the parking lot, getting supper ready, sharing a memory with a family member, or undressing before going to bed—during all those brief *everyday times*, I'll have in the *background* the formative images that shape my story during my teen years.

It's about *feelings*. Each *picture* in my life story has feeling attached to it. I might look long and hard at that image of myself on the playground in fifth grade. Feelings come to the surface if I let them—or, the picture of myself in that relationship in my early twenties. We know there are feelings there. There are powerful feelings associated with the birth of a child, the death of a loved one, the change of jobs, terrible family crises, images that come to mind throughout my marriage, battles with people I've struggled with. My feelings will help me *see* and *experience* how these pictures tell my story, who I am today.

It's about *God's fidelity*. This isn't a sentimental journey. With every picture in my story, there is a grace offered to me as I *look for God's presence* there. If, throughout this week,

I imagine God's having been present there with me—even when I didn't notice or feel it at the time—that would be a tremendous grace unifying my life.

It's about *gratitude.* With every memory, every image and feeling, practice saying, "Thank you." Even the painful ones. Even if I was not grateful then. Even if it involved some bad stuff I did to myself or to others. The Lord was there, loving me. Let gratitude now touch and span throughout the story of my life.

It's about *a journey.* This is only the beginning. We have thirty-four weeks. We will move slowly. And all we need to do is give God just a little space to transform our everyday lives, a moment at a time.

For the Journey: Expect God to Work

Do you know what's good for you? Knowing and then doing what we know is good for us are two distinct things.

I know that jogging is very good for my body and spirit, but going over to the recreation center is not only a good idea but also something I don't always want to do.

Taking vitamins is good for us, the medical profession tells us. We are just beginning to believe them, but we don't all take them all the time. We resist those activities that do not give us immediately the feedback we desire. We might begin a diet Monday morning and Tuesday morning we step lightly on the scale hoping to find less of us there. We want results and pretty darn quick!

We begin these weeks of exercising our spirits according to the pattern given by God to us through Ignatius Loyola, accompanied also by this human resistance to what is good for us.

The first guide, then, is this: do not expect, look for, or demand progress. Enjoy and live the process, even though, as with physical exercise, you might not like doing it every day. As with a diet, you might have to give something up, like time, activity, or accomplishments. We allow God to give the increase, the insights, the progress. We begin expecting God to be busy laboring on our part of creation, which we have found quite unfinished as a work of art.

This is the first guide along the way; don't stop here; the journey is worth the expense. Go for it!

In These or Similar Words . . .

Dear Lord,

This seems easy, going back through the photo album of my life. Can I really call this prayer? I can go back to my earliest memories, of being a toddler. I wonder what connection this little child has to me?

As I move through my life, into school, learning to read and expanding my world, I can notice things in this album that I don't want to see. They are difficult memories that cause pain and I thought I had put them away permanently. Not everything in my childhood was good. Where were you in that, Lord? Were you with me as I watched the shouting, the arguing?

There were good times, too. Running so freely as a kid, climbing trees, exploring the banks of the creek, and sledding down the big hill in winter. There is a freedom to those moments and I sense you in that, too.

As I got older, I made choices, Lord. For some of them, I ignored you completely and tried to pretend you didn't matter in my life. But you stayed with me so faithfully anyway. You guided my headstrong decisions into choices that helped me into a loving life and a good marriage.

Thank you, Lord, for your constant presence in my life, especially today.

Dear Lord,

I feel a little uncomfortable. This kind of prayer is new to me and I'm a little more comfortable using someone else's words. But I tried it yesterday and it wasn't hard; it just didn't always feel like prayer.

I return today and I look at the places where it hurts, the memories that make me want to squirm, pull away, and try to forget again. It hasn't always been easy in my life. Were you really with me in all of it? I feel you so strongly now, but I never thought much about you during those times.

How have these difficult times shaped me into what I am today? How has your faithful guidance helped me, unseen, over the years? Please help me to see your presence in my life and to be guided by it.

Scripture Readings

Luke 12:22–34
Isaiah 43:1–4
Luke 11:1–13
Psalm 8
Psalm 139

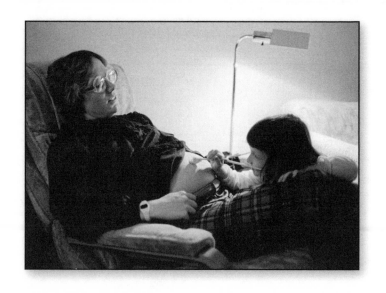

You created every part of me,
knitting me in my mother's womb.
For such handiwork, I praise you.
Awesome this great wonder!
I see it so clearly!

—Psalm 139:13–14

(*The Psalter*,
International Committee
on English in the Liturgy)

Our Story: Exploring Its Depth

Guide: Looking Closely at Our Stories

As we reviewed the photo album of our life stories last week, we all experienced special memories that have put us in touch with our God's presence with us throughout our life's journey. Our exercises this week will help us enter more deeply into our stories.

One powerful way to go deeper is to ask, and explore the answers to, key questions. We are still going to be doing this in the midst of our busy lives this week, and will keep utilizing the background (see the "Some Practical Help for Getting Started This Week" section). These questions are easy to remember and are important in preparing for the weeks to come. We were all "knit together in our mother's womb," as Psalm 139 tells us. Various events and experiences have shaped us into the people we are today. Let's listen for the answers that will reveal the depths of God's movement in us this week.

What graces, insights, special or painful memories
were given to me last week?

Did I like doing these exercises last week,
and did they nurture some new desires in me?

After last week's review of my photo album,
I'm attracted to . . .

Where, in my life story, did I feel most
totally known by God?

Is there a part of me, my story,
I have a hard time imagining God knowing?
Because I have a hard time imagining God
accepting me there?

Where in my story were there *crossroads*?
It could have gone this way or that:
how was God present in the way my story
continued from there?

Am I accepting of who I am today?
If not, can I hold those areas up to God?
If yes, can I hold my whole self up to God,
in gratitude?

Are there areas I feel God is wanting to
      love in me?
      change in me?
      make use of for others?

Throughout this week, in every background moment, let there
be expressions of gratitude for the blessings of how my life
story is connecting me with God's presence and love. Let me
experience the feeling of my continuing to grow and develop.
The one who formed us in our mother's womb is still forming
us this week.

Some Practical Help
for Getting Started This Week

Notice what the questions are about this week. That will make them memorable. They ask us to *focus* on images, memories, crossroads, specific painful memories. We could say, "I already *did* that!" This week we are asked to recollect those special memories that came to the surface and to revisit them, so that we can use them to go deeper.

Is there a *desire* coming out of last week? We'll see this question often. It asks us to be attentive, to *notice*, even the most subtle of new attractions, even new curiosities within me. For example, I might recognize a desire in me to spend more time reflecting on a particular time in my life that I didn't have much time to reflect on last week. Or I might just remember several important people in my life whom I haven't contacted in a while and feel a desire to write them.

Stay where you find fruit. This direction from Ignatius is very wise. If I've experienced *fruit*—consolation, some wonderful insight, a closeness to God, even a new awareness—I can trust that that *gift* is a *signal* from God: *"Look deeper here, my dear friend, for I have so much more I want to give you."* Another way of looking at this is to imagine receiving a gift, all wrapped in paper and ribbon and a big bow. I can know it's a gift, and even know who the giver is, and even say, "Thank you," without *opening it.* This direction from Ignatius invites us to *explore* the gift and discover what it really is.

Panning for gold. The image of panning for gold will be a helpful image throughout our retreat. Imagine a stream, with water rushing by all the time—a pretty good image of our busy lives. Imagine putting my pan—a sieve or screen—into the water. What happens? I get a pan full of stuff. As I shake it a bit, some of the smaller debris falls through the screen and I can look at larger stones that were in the water. And there in my pan, I discover a piece of gold. The message: I won't get that piece of treasure by just sitting by the edge of the stream peering into the water. I have to *pan* for it—sort out some portion of my experience and go deeper into it. And remember, if I discover some kernel of gold, it would be very important to *weigh* it—write it down and perhaps share the grace with others on the sharing page on the retreat Web site.

How NASA handles an image from space. Another image is that this is like the way NASA receives an image from space. When they first receive the image, it is fuzzy and one piece of a whole series of images. Then NASA gets to work to *clean up* the images—getting rid of the distortions that come from the long transmission. They then *digitally enhance* the image—basically, by filling in what is missing and thus making the image sharper. And finally, they put the various images together, and before our eyes, there is a spectacular Martian landscape.

It's still about background. Doing this retreat in everyday life will challenge us to keep using that space in the background. There's lots of debris and noise and distortion in our busy lives. If we can purify the background and let this week's questions flow in and out of that background all week, then we will notice a tremendous difference. Again, writing my answers down, or even saying them *out loud*, even in my head, will help preserve the grace.

By the end of the week we will want to be holding our whole life up to God—especially the parts that are least attractive, which might seem unacceptable. It's all about gratitude. I don't have to be *together* to be grateful.

Enjoy the journey. We are just beginning, starting to let God work in us. God can do infinitely more than we can ask or imagine. Let's trust it and enjoy it.

For the Journey:
Watching for What God Reveals

Our prayer during this retreat centers our attention on a loving God who centers affectionate attention on us. Two simple points of the nature of love help us pray during these weeks of praying with and about creation.

Love urges being revealed. If we love someone, sooner or later we will want that person to know. We might send a valentine and then a box of candy and then perhaps make a phone call and then get together. All the time there is a creative, ongoing revelation that presents the beloved with the opportunity to receive the affection or not. The lover wants his or her love to be experienced and received.

Love must be expressed in words and gestures that the beloved can understand. The lover must reverence the beloved so much that he or she adapts the expression of love to the way the beloved can receive it. If I love a blind person, I do not speak to them in sign language. If I love a German-speaking person, I don't speak any other language to that person except German. The lover adapts to the person and personality of the beloved.

In praying these next weeks, we watch how the loving God reveals that love through gestures of revelation. We also consider how this God adapts that same love to our ways of reception. We pray with God's courtship of us, constantly attracting us through acts of gentle yet persistent love.

We begin by considering that each of us has been and actually is now being created. God does not create us and then set us on the earth as so many abandoned milk jugs or degenerating cars. God tends to us as the beloved and labors on and around us for our soul's purpose. God wants only this, then: that we experience infinite love being revealed within our finite experiences and our reception of that love in our lives.

Our having been created tells each of us how important we are in the eyes of God, and our prayer these next weeks helps us to see our value and significance in our own eyes. In so many ways God says, "Look around and see who I have said and I say that you are." We are in the presence of a God who cannot keep love hidden, and we are God's best work of art.

In These or Similar Words . . .

Dear Lord,

Last week brought powerful, unexpected memories. When I prayed with the photo of the mother holding the child, I thought of the love you have for me, and the way you hold me close, protecting me from harm. It's an image I sometimes struggle against because I like to be free and independent, not needy.

Now as I pray with this week's photo, I think of your individual care for me, as an individual. I look at the young girl listening to the child in her mother's womb and I am flooded with a sense of the love and care you had for me even before I was born. The words in the Psalm move me: "You created every part of me, knitting me in my mother's womb." How can it be possible for you to have that much love for me—then and now?

I go back to places in my photo album that I looked at last week, places where I really felt you so strongly in my life. Isn't it odd that most of those times really are the difficult, painful ones? Why is it that I don't turn to you in the joy and the triumphs? Is it then that I delude myself into thinking that I'm in control of my life? That I don't need to rely on you—or anyone else?

When everything is going well, I have this vision in my head that I have to be perfect for you—and I'm not perfect. So I wait to really turn to you, thinking I will somehow correct all my flaws, by myself, before I come before you to speak.

But I look again at the photo album. When I'm in pain or in trouble, I fly to you for help. Later, when the pain eases, I don't always go running back to you. You are there waiting patiently, but somehow I keep thinking that I need to be a better person before I turn to you with my life. If I can just fix this one thing about myself—if I can just make this part of me better—that's when I will turn this all over to God. Suddenly I am aware, dear Lord, that now, in all of the things that are wrong in my life, in all of the things that I want to make better, now is when I need to turn to you.

Please hold my hand and go with me to the places inside me where I am afraid. Be with me as I look at myself with all of my flaws. Stay with me when I am afraid of my anger, my sadness, and my grieving for the pain in my life. It's the part I want to avoid the most, and yet it's where I need your love the most.

Thank you; thank you for being with me today, this week, and always. I am so grateful for your love and care. Help me to know how to repay your love.

Scripture Readings

Isaiah 49:14–16
Hosea 11:1–4
Psalm 23

In the beginning God created the heavens
and the earth.

—Genesis 1:1

Perspective—
A Picture of Harmony

Guide: The World as It's Meant to Be

After two weeks of reviewing our story, and seeing it as a story of God's faithful presence in our lives, we move now to look at the bigger picture.

This week we want to reflect on, and be inspired by, God's creative desire for us as part of the whole of creation.

St. Ignatius of Loyola put it so simply:

> *God created us*
> *to praise, reverence, and serve God*
> *and in this way to save our souls.*
> *God created all of the rest of creation*
> *to help us achieve the purpose for which*
> *God created us.*

Let's let the background of this whole week be two wonderful imaginative reflections:

- To simply walk around, doing all that I do each day, more and more conscious of why I was created:

    To give praise to God.
    To revere God: to grow in awe and love for God.
    To be of service: in God's service.

- To *notice* the rest of creation more consciously, and how all that I notice is intended by God to help me—it is all created for me.

Again, this is about *gratitude*. We want to *appreciate*, to become more *sensitive to* and more *aware of* something about God: God has an intense desire to help us achieve the end for which God lovingly created us. So, by our thinking and watching this week we are coming to know God better.

Again, make use of the helps provided for this week. Let the photo draw us into wonder and awe and a sense of God's plan for us. Let's try to begin and end each day this week with openness and delight in all that God intensely desires to show us.

Some Practical Help for Getting Started This Week

For Week 3, our perspective changes. Notice the dramatic view in this week's photo. It gives us a picture of how to get started with this week.

It's about *perspective*. This week, we will try to step back and see the whole view of ourselves in creation. So, throughout the week, let that picture of an expanding view of our world help us with perspective. This week, try not to let anything become *too big* and mess up our perspective.

It's about *purpose*. Concrete focusing can help greatly. Throughout the week, think of what things are *for*. We know what our coffee cup is for, what the toaster is for, what paper clips are for, what the telephone is for. As we consciously focus on the purpose that everything in our lives has, we will gradually feel the growing power of the words of Ignatius. It's all here for the purpose of helping me attain the end for which I was created.

Remember what we are *practicing*. We want to grow in the ability to find, see, experience, some connection with God *in all things*—and right in the midst of our busyness. So, we keep focused on practicing the use of the *background* times each day. Perhaps this week I can especially focus on *going to places*. So, on the way—to a meeting, to the restroom, to my lunch, to my car—I will consciously reflect on my *purpose*. *With practice*, I can situate myself, in a brief few moments, on that overview site from the photo. En route to the restroom, in my mind I'll be sitting on one of those chairs and looking out, thinking, *I was created, as part of this whole vast creation, for the one purpose of praising, reverencing, and serving you, Lord.*

Remember the other helps *from past weeks*. Naming graces is important. Saying *thank you* is critical. Try to *say it*—what is it that I'm receiving this week? "Lord, thank you for showing me the big picture." "Lord, thank you for reminding me about your desires for me."

Remember *our bodies*. What *posture* best says what I want to express? For example, I may imagine myself *standing* on that overlook in the photo and *raising my arms up* in praise. Then, perhaps, when I get out of bed and when I am ready to get into bed, I can raise my arms in praise that way, for only a moment. Or, maybe, as I look out over that vista, I imagine feeling drawn to kneel in awe before this God who is so much grander than I ever let God be. Perhaps I can kneel at the side of my bed for a brief moment. Or maybe I will imagine myself sitting on one of those chairs looking out at this creation, and I just open my hands on my lap, symbolizing my openness to be of service, as I am called. Then, perhaps, when I begin work each day, I might lay my open hands on my desk, or kitchen counter, for just a moment. These are powerful gestures that help us *interiorize* what we are expressing with our bodies— and they take only a few moments.

Remember to make use of the readings and prayers.

We are just beginning to see what God can do with our openness and trust.

For the Journey: The Foundation

A basement, or the basis or base of a building, is also the foundation of that building. In the Spiritual Exercises Ignatius begins with a most basic foundational statement. It is a simple formula but not always easy to accept. "Human beings are created." Each one of us is always being created by God's grace and the experiences that come from living our lives each day.

One of the more difficult factors to accept in being created is that we are limited; we have actual limitations of all kinds. We have age, size, abilities, personality, and gifts, but they are all limited by our not being God. We are who and what we are by God's creative love. Ignatius begins where we wish we might get to in time and with God's care.

Why we are being created is the second major section of this "basement platform." Ignatius was aware of the many answers humanity had proposed for this huge question. He had accepted that there is a God and that he is, and we are, creatures, but now the next big question had to be solved. How he answered these big questions and how we are invited to answer them determined the style of his life and will fashion ours. For Ignatius the answers to these big questions were simple, but it was far from easy to live them. With our limited selves, we are created to praise God for who God is as infinite Creator, and for creating each of us with these sometimes-hard-to-accept limitations. We are created as well to serve this creating God with and through the gifts we have been given—of course, through and with these same limitations.

No gift is meant just for ourselves; instead, they are gifts from God to me and through me to God's creating family.

The third aspect forming the major section of this basement is that, to serve in praise this God, we must reverence creation, which possesses God's fingerprints. Reverencing God will become a way of living by our becoming aware of the very holy presence of God in all other creatures. The challenge in our prayer is to be freed to reverence our own limitations enough so that, in our life given to serve God, we gratefully allow those limitations to be public, yet prophetic.

In These or Similar Words . . .

Dear Lord,

Today as I reflect on the world around me, it feels like gratitude is the first thing that comes to my mind. In the retreat this week I am trying to simply *notice* my life, to really see all of the wonderful gifts of nature that cross my path. Coming to work this morning, I couldn't help staring into an incredible sunrise through the cloudy sky. It created colors that were indescribable. A small tree in my yard is already turning colors, with bright red leaves that contrast with everything else that is still green. My tomato plants are still bearing fruit and the fall flowers are starting to line my sidewalk.

I see these as gifts to us—*us*—but I'm not sure I've ever really seen them as a gift from you to *me*. How can I fathom the depths of your love for me—that you have created each flower, each leaf, for my enjoyment? I'll be honest, God. I usually don't tune into this kind of thing. I just don't always pay attention to the gifts of nature that are literally under my feet.

Now as I pray, as I pay attention, I am moved by the phrase in the prayer guide this week, "God has an intense desire to help us achieve the end for which God lovingly created us." Could you really have a real desire for *my life*? For what becomes of *me*, not just as one of the billions of people who inhabit this planet, but as an individual?

I look outside at nature and inside at the family and friends you surround me with and I am so thankful. Please, Lord, help me to fully express my gratitude to you for my life and for the way you care for me. Help me to see what your desire for my life really is. I want to make my life a way to serve you.

Scripture Readings

Ephesians 1:3–12
Psalm 138

I am not complaining about having too little.
I have learned to be satisfied with whatever I have.
I know what it is to be poor or to have plenty,
    and I have lived under all kinds of conditions.
I know what it means to be full or to be hungry,
    to have too much or too little.
Christ gives me the strength to face anything. (CEV)

—Philippians 4:11–13

A Picture of Harmony— Living in Balance

Guide: Models of Freedom

This week we move from giving thanks and praise to God— from the big picture of ordered, purposeful creation—to the concrete picture of living in that harmony of purpose, in balance.

Throughout this week, we desire to be *inspired by* women and men who seem to be in harmony with the end for which we are created and who seem to use all of creation with this freedom.

St. Ignatius put it so simply:

We should use God's gifts of creation however they help us in achieving the end for which we were created, and we ought to rid ourselves of whatever gets in the way of our purpose.

In order to do this we must make ourselves indifferent to all creation, to the extent that we do not desire health more than sickness, riches more than poverty, honor more than dishonor, a long life more than a short life, or anything at all in and of itself. We should desire and choose only what helps us attain the end for which we were created.

We all know what a handicap it is to lack the indifference, or balance, in our lives that Ignatius talks about. When my *desire and choice* moves in the direction of "I want my health; I want success; I want to take care of myself; I crave honor and attention," I know I'm not in much balance and I'm becoming too self-absorbed.

However, when we see someone who seems to be carefree in loving, in giving of themselves, in living freely for others, we are *inspired*. That person seems to have gotten it right.

Let this week be one of naming and being inspired by people who seem to be models of freedom for me. As always, make use of the photo and the resources for this week. Look back at past resources if you'd like. But, in the everyday busyness of our week, we can let ourselves be conscious of the ways people live lives of praise, reverence, and service, perhaps heroically, perhaps in profound simplicity. Who are the people who show us the way to getting it right ourselves?

Some Practical Help for Getting Started This Week

Who are the people who show us the way to getting it right ourselves?

A very practical way to get started this week is to get out a piece of paper and make a list of the people who inspire me. Start with people I don't know. They can be people in history—a St. Ignatius or St. Teresa of Ávila or Martin Luther King Jr. They can be people I've at some time been inspired by—that guy who owned the textile plant out east, who, when his plant burned down, kept all his employees on the payroll until he could rebuild the plant. Then name the people I know personally who inspire me—it could be that great-aunt who lived a heroic life or my pastor or someone I love.

Once we've come up with this list of people, we can spend our week reflecting on *what qualities in each of them* inspire us. How is their life in balance? What is it that they seem to be *free from*? What is it that they are *free for*? What were or are their *choices and desires*?

The young woman in the photo for this week was one of our students here at Creighton University. She is in one of our mountain-village *campo* clinics in the Dominican Republic. Just look at her face this week. What is she feeling in her heart? It took only a little freedom to go down there, but we can see how in her service she is receiving far more than she is giving.

This is not a week for judging ourselves. We may become more aware of the unfreedoms in our lives, but it is not a time to become self-focused. There will be time later to let all these graces work together for our own spiritual freedom. This is simply the next step in our journey. Admiration precedes imitation. This is a week to walk around with a growing gallery of images of inspiring people, with qualities and dedication that show us the power of freedom.

Remember to let this process fill the background of our lives this week. Upon waking, putting on my slippers or my robe—for the briefest of moments—I can say a simple prayer of desire: "Lord, I want to be inspired this week. Let this day draw me closer to how people live their lives in great freedom." When I'm driving or walking down the hall or preparing dinner or perhaps as I'm reading the paper, someone on my list is in my mind, and some part of their grace-filled way of living is touching me. When I go to bed, perhaps as I'm turning out lights in the house, I can say, "Thank you, Lord, for those moments that stirred my heart today."

Check in with our progress throughout the week. How many people on my list have I reflected on? Do new names come to me? It will be difficult to keep focused this week. It is easier for us to be negative than to give ourselves over to sustained admiration. If I find myself losing focus this week, just return to these pages and refocus. Act against any negativity by returning to the photo.

Remember to say "thank you" throughout this week.

For the Journey: True Freedom

We are facing a prelude or overture this week, which follows the pattern of the *Spiritual Exercises*. It is like the opening section of a musical play, which gets us familiar and comfortable with the score that will be developed later in the work.

The difficulty with what we hear as openers this week can make us a bit uncomfortable and question whether we want to continue. Near the beginning of the Exercises, Ignatius displays what he means by freedom. I know that each of us wants a long life, health, a good name, and sufficient wealth. It may appear that right here, after such gentle prayer, the other shoe has finally dropped. To continue making these exercises, we must already have complete detachment from such natural desires and from life, health, and wealth.

In truth, Ignatius points to the universal human inclinations, which, if not tended to, can drive, dominate, imprison, and destroy our experience of life. We are invited in this overture simply to look at the areas that most commonly take us out of harmony. For the first time in this retreat we are asked to check whether we are free enough to face our unfreedoms. It is only when we do this that the rest of the symphony of the Exercises will make any sense.

We must be very clear about this, then; Ignatius assumes that as human beings we will experience disordering tendencies. Can I be honest and gentle with the uncovering of what plays such a loud part in my personal orchestra—that there is disorder in my life's symphony? Later, Ignatius will be inviting us to watch Jesus as the conductor of our own, and the world's, musical play. When Ignatius uses the term *indifference*, he does not mean "not caring." He is literally *up front* about where we are all going by making this retreat. Here, he indicates the areas of "over-caring" that will take us away from trusting in the God-caring that is true freedom. Will we, in time, be freed to watch, listen to, and follow the Divine Conductor?

This week we are guided toward a freedom that will be the result of honest reflection and prayerful surrender, but that takes time and God's good grace. The basic freedom of this week is the simple recognition of our human tendencies, which, when softened by our contact with Jesus and God's ways, become elements of harmony and balance. "Be not afraid"; the God who calls is faithful, and that God is constantly inviting us into the symphony of life.

In These or Similar Words . . .

Dear Lord,

It was easier last week. I looked at the balance and harmony in the world. I could see it in the changing of the seasons and the sunrise and in lots of wonderful things that didn't risk anything from me.

But now—now I'm being invited to look at the harmony, or lack of it, in my own life. I was so struck by the words in the guidepost: "Can I be honest and gentle with the uncovering of what plays such a loud part in my personal orchestra—that there is disorder in my life's symphony?" Something in me is stirred by that, Lord. There are parts of me that are too loud in the symphony of my life. I hear the horns too loudly as I worry about failing or about being seen as a failure. Drums are banging as I am too attached to the admiration of others, and it feels shallow because all I want is to somehow give my life to you.

Please, Lord, I beg you. Give me the grace to see how to balance my life. How can I have the kind of calm and peace that the woman in the photo this week has? She is sitting in a poor clinic and laughing in the midst of the tragedy around her. The peace she has doesn't have anything to do with money, pride, or how other people see her. She has given her life to you. Help me find that kind of peace in my own life.

But then I get afraid. What are you asking of me, Lord? How much do I have to give up? Can I do this? I am so torn between wanting my life to be in balance and in harmony with you and not wanting to give up anything that I now have. I'm just afraid. In my fear I turn to you and open my arms, asking for the help I need.

Please, God, help me live my life in a way that draws me closer to you. Help me give up anything that doesn't do that. Thank you so much for your love and your care for me. Thank you for creating me and desiring me to be in harmony with you.

Scripture Readings

Ephesians 2
Romans 8
Matthew 10:29–31

Take this, all of you, and drink from it:
this is the cup of my blood,
the blood of the new and everlasting covenant.
It will be shed for you and for all
so that sins may be forgiven.

—Eucharistic Prayer

The Disorder of Sin—
Appalling Rebellion

Guide: What Sin Is

We have spent several weeks enjoying what it is to live in harmony with our purpose and to be inspired by people who seem to get it right. We now turn to look at another picture. Fr. Doll's photo of a bombed Bosnian village can symbolize for us both the revolting evil that results from the rejection of God and God's desire for us and for humanity.

Why do we go here this week? We want to see, to taste, *what sin is*—an appalling rebellion against God. This is not to look at some vague sense of social evil, without any responsible villains. Our intention is to spend this week more consciously aware of the *sheer arrogance* and *outrageous opposition* to God's grace that exists in our world. Why? We do this because we rarely look evil in the face, and we do this that we might more deeply come to know the loving mercy of our God, in the death and resurrection of Jesus for the sin of the world.

So, there are really two images this week:

1. The ones that will come to us this week that represent the sin of the world.

2. The image of Jesus on the Cross, liberating us from sin and death's threat of victory over us.

The enemy of our relationship with God does not want to be *unveiled* by our staring at, our becoming wiser to, just what sin is. This is not primarily about our *personal sin*, though we are all sinners. Our desire this week is to grow in what our culture seems to have lost—*a sense of sin*.

From time to time this week, we look back though history and let our imagination picture all of the violence, the inhumanity, the injustice, the abuse, the greed, and the lust for power—humanity in rebellion from God's desire that we praise, reverence, and serve God and use everything else in creation for that end.

How much denial of God's right to praise, reverence, and service can we experience this week? How much worshipping of other gods? How much violence against the dignity of human life? How much deception or injustice or scandal or depravity? We want to experience the *magnitude* of the sin of the world, so we don't hesitate to explore its scope.

Our goal is not to become judgmental and to grow in anger at sinners. Our desire is to experience the *ingratitude* and *prideful independence* from God that sin represents. It is *disorder*, and we are feeling *how wrong* it is.

Each day this week, our consciousness of evil would be too great for us to bear without the second image: *God's loving, merciful response.* The price for it all is paid for in the body and blood of Jesus, there on the cross.

We end each day with growing gratitude for the *magnitude* of God's Mercy.

Some Practical Help
for Getting Started This Week

This is an important week to see that there is a natural progression to our retreat. These exercises build on the graces of the previous weeks, just as the upcoming weeks will build on the graces of this week. This week we will be reflecting on some realities that we normally don't reflect on. Here are some practical suggestions for making this week more fruitful.

Pay attention to the beginning and ending of each day. This remains *key* to our being able to stay focused each day. As I wake each day, and put on my slippers or robe—for a very brief few moments—I will recall the grace I desire today: to enter more deeply into a sense of what sin really is. I may say, for example, "Lord, let me see and feel the outrage of the evil that seems to reign in our world. Lord, I so want to be moved by the profound depth of your love and mercy." At the end of each day, let all these images be replaced by the one image of Jesus on the cross. Each night, try to return to that image. Try to let it become more real. Perhaps I can imagine looking up into the face of Jesus and speaking to him my gratitude. Perhaps I will imagine speaking face-to-face with our risen Lord, as he is today, asking him to show me the holes in his hands and feet and side today, as they remain the signs of the power of God's love.

The content will take some effort this week, but it will be worth it. The photo of the horror of Bosnia can be the entryway into all the other appalling evils of our world. I think of all of the wars in history and the atrocities committed for the sake of some leader or because of people's lust for power. I think of all the innocent children, deprived of even a chance to experience human freedom and dignity. I imagine systemic corruption and the resulting cost to all of humanity. I remember loved ones and friends who are real victims of sin. Perhaps I have experienced the tragedy of caregivers who failed to love or the betrayal of a loved one.

How does this *grief*, or even *outrage*, become the *background* of my everyday life this week, without affecting my mood, my attitude at work or with my family? We do want it to affect our hearts. We want to take our blinders off and really see and feel the power of evil. But *at the same time*, we want to experience the power of God's response. This week should not *discourage* us. It should give us *hope*.

This week will be a great grace if we keep mindful of the focus: asking for the grace to see the outrageous, rebellious evil of sin in the world and the merciful love of God in the death of Jesus for the sin of our world.

Writing down a grace, sharing it with another, e-mailing someone, or sending it in to be shared here are all ways to deepen the experience.

Perhaps by midweek we can ask ourselves how we are doing. We can ask, "Is it difficult for me to look at *the evil of the sin of the world*? To be outraged by it? Is it difficult for me to grow in gratitude for the mercy of God?"

For the Journey: Praying with Sin

Praying with sin, whether it be our own or that of our world, does not invite a joyful response from us at first. As someone once said, "There's nothing original about sin." None of us likes to consider the damage of hurricanes or the destruction of wars. The more sensitive one is, the more he or she shrinks from viewing or imagining the ugliness of violence and hatred.

In praying about sin in the Exercises, the main question is whether guilt is a grace or a tangent. Perhaps I could put it this way: Does a painting receive anything from its frame? The frame should lead the eye to what it frames, obviously. In considering the rebellion and ingratitude of sin, what is the picture and what is the frame?

For most of us, our participation in the sin of the world and our own personal sins fill the whole canvas, and the surrounding frame is the somewhat arbitrary love of Jesus for this world and for us.

The opposite is true for those praying these considerations of the Exercises. Always the main central picture is the love of Jesus Christ for us and for our world. What highlights this love is the deep reality of our resistance to live in and trust that love. Our sin is why Jesus came to take his place in the center of the canvas of history.

My father was a lawyer and his firm's motto was "The worst injury is the one not properly represented." Our worst sins are those we hold to ourselves, refuse to recognize, and do not allow Jesus to take into the center of his cross. He does more than represent us; he re-presents us back into the world that he loves and offers us as a healing gift.

There is a proper grace of guilt when it remains the frame and leads us to consider and then receive the freeing forgiveness of Jesus. Guilt is a distracting tangent when we consider that it leads us to put ourselves at the center of our unforgiveness. We can spin our spiritual wheels in the muck and mire of our own self-destruction, and in doing so, we hope that God will see how much punishment we are inflicting on ourselves so that God just has to have pity on us. That puts God not at the center, but far outside the frame of our lives. God is neither a spectator nor an art critic.

The real freedom to which the Spiritual Exercises calls us is the freedom to let God be God and to allow us to be loved not only as we are now but also as we will be. In praying this week, can we be honest but not negative?

In These or Similar Words . . .

Dear Lord,

I'm confused. For the past four weeks, I've prayed with these beautiful photos, of mothers, children, landscapes, and happy people, and in my prayer I have felt love and harmony. But this week, there is only a bombed-out village—such a stark picture that jars the rhythm of the others. I know you are there in the love and harmony. Are you also there in the destruction?

I almost don't know how to pray when I look at the photo. I want to pray for the people who have lost their families and their homes, whose lives have been changed because of this. I want those people to find support from you, some impossible peace in their shattered lives.

But as I look at the photo, I wonder about those who have become so separated from you that they carry out this kind of destruction against their brothers and sisters. What is it that leads us as humans to treat each other this way? What must that be like for you, God, to watch us, the people you created, destroy each other?

I think of my own family and how I would feel if I spent a lot of time making a gift for my daughter, thinking of how it would make her happy and please her. What if she looked at it, said "thanks," and then tossed it in the closet? What would that be like for me? Is it presumptuous to wonder what the same thing is like for you, God?

Help me this week to feel how sin is a rejection of you. Help me break through the resistance I have to look at anything evil. Stretch me to appreciate how sin is nothing more than ingratitude to you, who creates life and gives it purpose and meaning. I want to disdain evil the way I disdain anything that hurts me. I want to have the instinctive sense of how selfishness destroys and subverts your purpose and plan.

And when I look up at you on the cross, help me to feel, help me to sense how you embrace and take upon yourself all of this evil. How do I say "thank you" to you? Let me never take for granted how your selfless gift saves me from the destruction of sin and death.

Scripture Readings

Colossians 2:9–15
Psalms 10 and 73
1 John 1:5–2:2
Luke 15:1–10

Christ died for us at a time when we were helpless and sinful. No one is really willing to die for an honest person, though someone might be willing to die for a truly good person. But God showed how much he loved us by having Christ die for us, even though we were sinful.

—Romans 5:6–8

The Disorder of Sin— Personal Rebellion

Guide: A Time for Deep Self-Knowledge

After King David had an affair with Bathsheba and had her husband, Uriah, killed, Nathan the prophet came to him with a parable. A rich man, who had many sheep, stole the one sheep his poorer neighbor had. David was filled with outrage at the evil deed of the rich man. Nathan then told David, "You are that rich man!"

Whenever we look at the terrible sin of the world, for which Jesus died on the cross, we must pause and explore that same rebellion from God in our own hearts.

The grace we turn to God for this week is that we might *know* our sin—completely and profoundly—so that we might know the *depth* of God's love for us personally. We want to know our sin at the level of our feelings.

What have I done? What have I failed to do? Habitually? Almost instinctively? At each stage of my life? When, throughout my life, to this very day, have I acted independently of God? When did I make up my own rules? How have I been dishonest—to others, to myself? When was I cruel or abusive?

Lustful and greedy in my desires for power, control, consumption, self-gratification? To what degree have I rationalized and made excuses? How have I let my heart become *cool* to God and to others?

What evil continues because of me? Who remains hurt or damaged because of my selfishness? How have I been deaf to the cry of the poor? By not wanting to get involved or convincing myself that it wasn't my responsibility? How have I *insulated* myself, lived in my own world, so that I don't get *bothered* by the needs of others? How does my *comfort* cost others? How have I failed to notice, to care, to investigate, to respond, to get involved, to seek change? Do the poor have me as an *advocate for them*?

This is time for deep self-knowledge with a growing desire to know, as never before, the *depth* of God's forgiveness and love. This should not be *depressing* but *liberating*. For we will discover that in our own ways we have *auctioned off* the cross and really strayed far from the desires God has for us. But we will end each day discovering that that cross signs a *wondrous love* that frees us from our sin.

This is indeed a week to say "thank you" and to say it with growing feeling. In brief moments, let's tell our risen Lord, Jesus, how grateful we are, in words, with more intimate affection.

The resources and helps will be very important this week. The readings and prayers are particularly rich. The online version of this retreat has a section called "A Place to Share," where people can go to share their reflections. Consider sharing your graces there, even anonymously.

Some Practical Help for Getting Started This Week

This is an important week for this retreat. It prepares us for the weeks ahead. We know it isn't an easy week, because it is so against the grain of our culture to examine our hearts before God.

As we begin, there are several important cautionary statements to make. First of all, if you are suffering from clinical depression, please make these exercises only with the guidance of a spiritual director. The whole purpose of this week is to experience *deep gratitude* for the profound depth of God's love and mercy for me. A director will help ensure that the week doesn't get out of focus.

For all of us, it should be noted that the very natural response to an unveiled exploration of our willful sinfulness is genuine *shame*. It is a real grace of this week, but only the *first part* of it. The second part is the surprising realization that I know God more intimately when I am overwhelmed with God's love for me there—*as* a sinner. The two graces go together. If I am determined to avoid the feeling of *shame*, I make it very difficult for God to give me the power of the second grace.

For those of us for whom past experiences of having been *shamed*, in its debilitating or even its abusive senses, has caused great damage to our sense of self, this grace needs to be experienced as *totally different* from that kind of destructive experience. The grace of this week can be very healing to a *shame-based* view of ourselves. For anyone who desires this healing, we strongly recommend proceeding with this retreat, with the assistance of a spiritual director.

That having been said, let's not be afraid to ask God to show us who we are—loved sinners. Let's explore some *methods* that might be helpful for this week.

How we begin is critical. We are asking for graces. That tells us, from the beginning, that we are not going to achieve what we desire on our own here. It will not be the result of *our work* alone. It will be a *gift*—a gift from God. So we begin asking for the grace to be led, guided, shown the way. I might ask God to shine a light on the areas God wants me to see. I might ask God to help me experience the times I have been rebellious, with emotion.

It may appear that doing this week *in the background* of my everyday life is more difficult, but it really isn't. I may want to work to find some times to remember and reflect. I may want to plan to have a lunch alone or to spend some extra time walking somewhere, or to just get up a half an hour earlier—by going to bed a half an hour earlier. The essential nature of this retreat remains the same—it's about unifying my day, from the time I awake to just before I sleep, with a sense of God's presence with me on this journey. It's about consciously focusing on what I'm doing this day, so that more and more of the *background* of my life changes.

Getting concrete is critical. Having a plan is important. For example, I may want to plan to explore the years of my youth early in the week, the middle part of my life during the middle of the week, and my life today at the end of the week. We don't want to have a *vague sense* of it all. We want to explore concrete actions, attitudes, consequences of my decisions, habits that I developed and didn't change, opportunities to love that I passed up, and ways I was deaf to the cry of the poor. Be concrete.

Some of us may be tempted to say that we didn't do a lot of bad things in our lives—we never had an affair or acted dishonestly in our jobs or acted in an unloving way to another person—and that we have always thought of the poor and given generously of our time and money and taught our children to do the same, so we haven't been a sinner. We may need to be more diligent in taking time to examine our heart for any hint of pride or judgment of others or lack of compassion for those who have a more difficult time being good. If we beg God to show us what it is we need to convict ourselves of, our *shame*, God will provide.

For some of us, it will be that really bad single sin or pattern of sin we are so aware of—whenever I think of sin I think of a long-standing habit of abusing alcohol or that affair about which I feel so guilty or a time when I seriously abused another or a person I simply hate or can't forgive. If this becomes the focus of our week, and becomes a way for God to show us love and mercy, it will be a profound grace. However, resist the temptation to stop there, with that single bad sin. Let's unveil our whole lives here. For most of us, the ways we are rebellious in our failures to praise, reverence, and serve God are often quite subtle. We want to know and experience God's love for us, not just because we did this or that. We want to experience love and mercy for who we are—who we have been and who we have become.

Finally, that takes us to Jesus. Let's end each day conversing with Jesus—pouring out our hearts, friend to friend—with growing gratitude.

Consider sharing the graces you received this week, either with someone close to you, or by using the Sharing pages on the online version of the retreat. And let's pray for one another.

For the Journey: The Redeeming Love of God

The dramatic sculpture of the Pietà, which resides inside St. Peter's Basilica in Rome, is safely behind glass now. It was, at one time, more accessible and vulnerable. The beautiful creation was attacked and damaged by a mentally injured fellow. Most of the world's great paintings are guarded and protected in similar manners. Why?

Sin is a part of the same creation that also brings us such beautiful works as paintings, statues, forests, rivers, and other human beings. We pray early and often during the Exercises about God's creative and sustaining relationship of love that God has for each and every creature. Very simply stated, sin is the action that flows from the attitude that my selfish, greedy, and irreverent relationship with any of God's creatures replaces God's own relationship with them. It all goes back to reverence and seeing God in everything and seeing everything in God.

Through my need for efficiency, I might have used a sterling-silver butter knife to pry open a paint can. Sin is not that I broke the knife, but the attitude of disrespect for the limitations of sterling silver that God placed there and gave to us. Sin is also my disregard for the importance to another human being of that piece of silver.

You may check out your behavior against the demands of the Ten Commandments and find that you haven't violated any of those. Sin is more relational than that. More important than the Ten Commandments are the personal covenants that God has made with us through all of creation. Sin is how we violate, ignore, and freely choose to replace God's prior relationship with an object or person with my own self-centered blueprint.

Ignatius offers us his picture of God as always working, laboring to attract and support us. God's mercy is above all other works. Mercy is not only his forgiving of our violations of God's covenants with us, but even more, God intensely desires us to come more and more alive, alert, aware, and sensitive to his presence in his presents. Forgiving us is God's judicial side, continuing our personal creation is his compassionate side.

Jesus did not give up on his friends or on those whom he found to be enemies. He was always speaking, working around, to have them all come to their full senses.

In praying this week in the frightening area of violent and irreverent sin, stay close to the image of Jesus on the cross. He is there to manifest both the evil of sin and the loving response of God to that evil. We can look at anything while standing next to the cross. The grace we seek this week is a gratitude for the ongoing, redeeming love of God that both cancels the debt against us and works that we might have life and have it to the full.

In These or Similar Words . . .

Dear Lord,

I don't want to look! Am I just like King David? I can be filled with outrage at the stories I read about the global issues about dictators, starvation, and the mistreatment of fellow human beings. How can they treat others that way? How can they let sweatshops continue or ethnic cleansing to go on? But now, as I pray, I see my own sinfulness beginning to emerge.

I don't think of myself as a sinner—not a real one. But here I am faced with some of my own shortcomings. I call them shortcomings! Look at me, Lord—I don't even want to admit they are sins! But they are. I see how judgmental I am of people, how quickly I decide whether people are worthy of my approval. I'm ashamed when I see how I have so many prejudices that I mostly try to ignore.

All of these awful things are a part of me. Lord, I almost want to run. How can I face you with such sins? But please, Lord, I beg you. I want to feel your love to the very depths of my being, and I know that first I have to feel your forgiveness. Show me my real self, with all of my flaws. It's not just the way I treat others. I can see it going deeper, Lord. What about the way I ignore others? I pretend I'm far too busy to really get involved with others. I tell myself I can't help it if they are poor or homeless. I have my own family to take care of, my own life to deal with.

Please, heal me. Help me to overcome the way I rebel against you. Heal my heart that resists loving other people and resists loving you. Show me how I choose to ignore you and your teachings. I sin against you and my brothers and sisters. Reveal my selfishness to me, my self-centeredness and self-absorption. Show me how my fears are a way to keep my distance from you.

Stay with me, Lord, and help me. Let me feel your love for me. Let me feel you soften the hardness of my heart. Fill and warm me with your love. Let me carry that love with me and let go of the hardness, the rebellion, the discord, the prejudices. Help me to be as open to others as I am open to your love. Today, tonight, let me embrace the cross that I so often auction off. Let me be helpless before you in gratitude for your wondrous love for me.

Thank you, Lord. Thank you for your endless love and for your bottomless forgiveness.

Scripture Readings

1 John 1:8–2:2
Luke 15
Luke 7:36–50
Luke 18:9–14
Luke 19:1–10
Psalm 51

Finally, I turn to the God who made me
and beg that I might embrace the freedom
being offered me.

—"Guide" for Week 7

The Disorder of Sin—
Personal Patterns

Guide: Uncovering the Mystery of Our Sin

Last week we reviewed the record of our sins in the light of God's love for us. This week we give ourselves the time to probe the *patterns* of our sinfulness that we might even more deeply understand God's love and desires for us.

We've all seen those children's puzzles that begin with a page full of dots. As we draw lines to connect the dots, an image appears that we couldn't see before. That's what this week is about.

We want to connect the dots and see the patterns emerge, so as to understand just how sin happens in us. What motivations come into play? What forces are in tension in my heart? Can I identify underlying *inclinations* that habitually and instinctively work against God's desires in me? Can I put names on my most basic *unfreedoms*? My most basic *fears*?

Sin, and the unfreedom that supports it, are complex realities. Nobody really gets up in the morning and says, "I think I'm going to be unloving today. I've decided to be selfish, in fact, just plain absorbed in myself today. Yes, whenever given the choice, I come first. I'm going to give in to lust and greed today, and I'm going to block out the cry of the poor; I just won't pay attention to my role in the rest of the world." We all know that it is much more subtle than that. We always sin by choosing something that we think is good, that we think is right for us, that we think we need. Our desire here is to uncover *the way* we approach sin.

Throughout this week, let's increase the intensity of our desire for God's help. Just as when I am approaching a critical surgery and ask *everyone I know* to pray for me, I might turn to loved ones who have died to ask them to intercede with the Lord for me, so that I might be given an instinctive insight into my sinfulness. I can feel them eager for my freedom. I might spend time with Mary, the mother of our Lord, and ask her to intercede on my behalf. I can surely feel that she is there for me. Then I can turn to Jesus directly, pouring out my gratitude for the graces already received in this retreat and begging him to ask God, the Father and our Creator, to give me the grace to see the sinful patterns in my life. Finally, I turn to the God who made me and beg that I might embrace the freedom being offered me.

The more deeply we comprehend the mystery of our sin, the more intensely we will feel that the mercy and love of the death and resurrection of Jesus is *for me.*

Some Practical Help for Getting Started This Week

Honesty, humble sorrow, and deep gratitude are graces we desire for this week. What concrete means can we use to open ourselves to receive these graces from our Lord, who deeply desires to give them to us?

First of all, it may be important to review last week's help, regarding some important cautions about doing these exercises without a director.

Penetrating focus is the key. Here are a few examples.

If one of the sins that I have remembered is that I had an affair a number of years ago, this is the week during which I can uncover all the grace that is being offered me. (Any serious sin offers the same opportunity.) The temptation here is to say that it is something I did in the past, it is over, I confessed it, I was forgiven, and I shouldn't dwell on it because it will never happen again. Why dredge up an old sorrow? This is a possible time for several new graces. I can beg to understand the pattern or patterns beneath the sin. I can ask to understand the underlying dishonesty and recklessness, even to explore the neediness and selfishness that was there. If I keep going, in the confident trust that God's love and mercy will show me a grace that reveals the depth of that love, God's grace will be given. Perhaps I will discover that the heart of this sin was not sex, for example, but an escape from myself, from the loneliness or pain I was feeling. Perhaps I will be given a grace to see, in this trusting exploration, that my deepest sin was that I failed to turn to the Lord in my need; I didn't rely on or even listen to what grace might have been offered me there. When I'm in trouble, I do something to fill the void, escape the pain, hide the mistake, compromise here and there. Perhaps I will see a pattern in my unwillingness to accept the cross in my life—dying to myself—because I haven't accepted the depth of the freedom offered to me in the Lord's dying on the cross for me. And what can draw me into this depth is the attraction to know the profound embrace of love that is offered me there, when everything is opened in the light of God's love.

If one of the areas I'm examining as a pattern this week is my failure to love in a variety of ways, this can be a powerful week to understand a complex rut I may be stuck in and to experience the graced desire to surrender my heart in grateful response to the love offered me. So, what lies beneath the limits I place on relationships? How about the way my friends and I securely judge, even attack, those others who we believe are sinners? What is the *unlove* that characterizes the traits that people see in me? What has been the basis of my coolness to becoming involved in service for the poor? It is in the answers to these questions that I will discover the graces being offered me. Here is where I will discover the need for deep healing of parts of me that seem deep rooted. Because I don't see myself as a big sinner, I can too often avoid looking at the patterns that prevent me from becoming an effective disciple of Jesus with all of my heart. Here is where I discover the Lord's desire for the rest of my heart. And, of course, it is here that I discover the depth of Augustine's prayer: "Oh, Lord, our God, you have created us for yourself, and our hearts are restless until they rest in you"—and, we might add, to rest in a wondrous love beyond what we can ask for or imagine.

Throughout this week, with whatever I discover, it will be important to keep drawing it together into an image of myself, loved by God. From time to time, if I penetrate the patterns deeply, I will discover an image of myself that is complicated, often inconsistent, very messy, quite unattractive to myself. I will be overwhelmed with the mystery of how God could *possibly* love someone who has been such an *unreliable servant*, someone who has had such a divided heart. Here is where God reveals himself. It is right here that we discover who we are and here that we discover our need for a savior.

A final image might help throughout this week, as we look at the photo of ourselves, deep in prayer. We can imagine our lives like a *house*. Our lives, like a house, often have nice front yards. We might even invest lots of money in presenting an impressive image when driving by. Just inside our house, there is an entryway and living room, where we greet and entertain most of the people who get into our lives. People who are more intimately involved in our lives get invited farther in as dinner guests, next-door neighbors or lifelong friends. And, of course, there are the intimate places in our house—the bathrooms and bedroom—where only the most intimate parts of our life happen. But in every house—in every life—there is a *basement* (or attic or garage) where the less-than-presentable stuff is kept. This week, we can imagine going down into that basement, even if there has been a lock on that door and I haven't visited it in a long time. I need not be afraid, because I'm going to go down there, accompanied by Jesus, who will show me all the stuff that is there. There's old stuff there I wouldn't want to show anybody else. There's embarrassing stuff there, in hiding. As I walk around it all, I can imagine Jesus telling me he loves me here, in this place. I can hear him tell me he loves *all of me—the whole me.*

Don't avoid this week for fear that it will be negative. That would avoid a tremendous grace. A *check* we can use throughout the week is to ask whether I am growing in a sense of God's love, in a sense of gratitude for that love, in a sense of myself as a loved sinner. Then the focus won't be on ourselves, but on the one who desires to fill our restless hearts.

For the Journey: Comfort in Our Discomfort

Praying about personal sin has several meanings. The prayer of it has to do with regaining a sense of how impersonal I have really been in my relationship with God and God's creatures. The gifts of my life have been given as a relational experience; God as person contacting me as person.

My personal pattern of sin is how I have objected to the personal contact from God and refused to see these gifts as from God, but simply as objects for my own conversation with myself.

Praying about my pattern of sin centers my attention on what fears, what needs, what circumstances, and what demands are operating when I lose contact with the personal gifts around and within me. Actions flow from attitudes, and such fears and hungers break out into acts that we can call personal sin, but they actually are impersonal as well. Simply stated, I forget or choose not to regard everything as personally offered by the personal God. We pray this week with Jesus personally encountering those people who are honest enough to admit their sickness, disability, and injury. Before Jesus can meet them in a healing way, they have to have met themselves in a humbling way. They have to have faced the truth of their own personal condition. In praying about our sin and patterns of being impersonal, we, like the prodigal son, have to come to our senses and return to ourselves first. Jesus meets those who have first met themselves.

It is extremely important for those considering the patterns of sin to do so while sitting at the feet of Jesus, where we can experience the personal touch of his compassionate eyes. To do such reflection on the patterns and history of our sin in isolation will lead only to further disgrace and self-rejection. Honesty is not humiliation, but a prelude to being engraced. True freedom is worth the time it takes to sit at his feet and be comforted in our discomfort.

In These or Similar Words . . .

Dear Lord,

Please. I'm not sure where to begin, but I think I need to begin with your love. If I don't feel that, I'm not sure I can go any farther. Here, I sit in the dim light, surrounded by my sins like mushrooms springing up in a damp forest. As I look closer, more and more of them seem to crop up. I review my life and see basic sins, but now as I look again, I see patterns to them and the same sin coming up over and over again.

Oh, Lord! The way I treat people, angrily, impatiently, always needing to be in control. My life seems to be ruled by the need to look good, and yet I know that inside there are so many parts that are small and selfish and very dark. What is it inside of me that makes me turn my back so completely on you and the love you hold out to me?

Please, Lord. I beg you. Let me feel the pain and alienation of being separated from you. Let me know what it really is to be disconnected from your love and to feel so very lost without you. Free me, my God. Free me from the attachments I cling to. Touch the parts of me that need so much healing. Touch the selfishness inside me that makes me forget how I long to be next to you.

Help me turn to others with more compassion and forgiveness, the same compassion and forgiveness you have held out to me with open arms so many times. How can I so easily be angry and unforgiving with others and then turn to you so automatically when I need forgiveness?

Hold me gently, Lord. Calm my heart, so frantic and disconnected from you. Teach me to cherish others as you cherish me. I have so often asked you to soften your heart toward my sin. Please, I ask you now to soften the hardness of my heart toward others.

I want to say to you as Peter did, "Lord, don't come near me! I am a sinner." But I know that you will turn to me, as you did to Peter, and say, "Don't be afraid."

Heal me. Hold me. Be with me, God.

Scripture Readings

Matthew 8:1–13
Luke 9:23–25
2 Corinthians 12:8–10
Luke 5:1–11
Luke 5:17–26
Matthew 25:31–46

"[This loved one of mine] was lost
and has now been found."
And they began to celebrate.

—Luke 15:24

God's Love for Us— Forgiving Mercy

Guide: How God Must Rejoice

This week we will walk around in God's love for us. We want to taste—to fully enjoy—the forgiveness that is God's gift to us.

Though we have been trying to end each reflection on sinfulness with the reality of God's mercy, during this week we will try to let God's merciful forgiveness fill the background of our entire week.

We begin by focusing on God. The photo of a mother's embrace of her daughter will inspire us throughout this week to keep our focus on God. This woman's face will help us to begin to imagine the powerful depth of God's embrace of us.

As I wake up, put on my slippers or robe each morning, and begin to get moving, I can focus, for a moment, on God's delight in me. *How God must rejoice in my coming to know how much I'm loved and forgiven!* As I go through each day, I can recall various images that help my spirit soar with accepting the intimacy of forgiving love's embrace.

I can imagine the joy I have experienced when a loved one's biopsy came back negative, or when friends found the child they were waiting to adopt, or when someone I care deeply about receives my love and enjoys it. *How much more God rejoices in us this week!*

We resist the temptation to figure out *how* God could forgive our sins, our patterns—all we have done and all we have failed to do. The answer to that question is wrapped up in the mystery of love—love without condition or limit. We might imagine forgiving a spouse or child or someone we love simply because our love is so much greater and stronger than the wrong that was done. *And we tell ourselves how much greater God's love for me must be, to forgive me so freely, so completely!*

There is a phrase we use to describe something so wonderful. We say, "It's *incredible*; I can hardly *believe* it!" This week we enter into our desire to not only believe God's forgiving mercy to me but also to experience it, accept it, and celebrate it. *How much that must be God's own desire for each of us this week!*

Use the resources that follow to enrich the week's retreat experience. You will find other resources on the Online Retreat Web site. Consider sharing the graces of this week there. We will never know how a gift given to us might truly help another.

Some Practical Help for Getting Started This Week

This is not an easy week for many of us. In the third parable of mercy, which Jesus tells to those who criticize his eating and drinking with sinners (Luke 15), the younger son's return to his father is full of remorse, "*I have sinned against God in heaven and against you. I am no longer good enough to be called your son.*" The older son is full of resentment that the father forgives the younger son so freely. And like the religious leaders that criticize Jesus, he won't join in the celebration. It is not easy for us to get beyond feeling terrible about our sin or the patterns of sinfulness in our lives. And even when we find ourselves in the embrace of Forgiving Love, there's an older brother's or sister's voice inside us, putting a damper on the celebration.

This is the week to surrender to God's embrace. Look at the photo over and over. Imagine being in that embrace. Stay there. Don't rush it. Let all the resistance melt away. Receive it. Enjoy it. Rest in it. What is the one who is embracing me feeling and expressing in that moment of togetherness? Throughout this week, whatever I'm doing, in those in-between times, I can close my eyes and imagine Jesus holding me like that.

This is the week to *smile*—to wear it on our face and to feel it deeply. A smile and a deep breath go together very well. They prepare the way for a joyful and wonderfully refreshing inner peace.

Do all the rest of my problems go away? Is my life back together? Have I reached the depths of spiritual freedom? Of course not. We keep reminding ourselves that this is a *journey*, and each week is an important *next step*. This is a critical next step—to experience and enjoy and celebrate, because I am a loved sinner.

Perhaps this week I can find several things to do that will lift my spirits and reinforce this week of enjoyment and peace. Plan it; make some change in the routine; give the week a different feel.

Most important, this week is about *gratitude and expressing it*. What am I *feeling* as I rest in that embrace? After all I have done and failed to do, and considering the patterns that still shape my life—to be forgiven so completely! How does that feel? If tears come forth, let them flow. How do I want to respond to the one who has loved me this much? I need to say those words in thanksgiving. To be forgiven is a tremendous gift. We want to express our gratitude in words that claim it and allow us to enter even more deeply into the joy and peace.

Rituals are important. They involve our bodies and *last* in our memories. Perhaps I will put my expression of gratitude on paper, in words that express all that I feel, addressing it directly to Jesus or to God. As I read "In These or Similar Words . . . ," I can find *my* words and say them out loud or put them in writing. For some of us, standing in the solitude of our room, with arms stretching up toward heaven, wonderfully expresses how we feel. For some of us, it will be important to recall a song that we sing to mark this very special week. Perhaps I will celebrate the Eucharist this week or on Sunday, or participate in my faith community's worship, with a deeper sense of joy.

The measure for each of us this week will be how we go to sleep each night. If I can put my clothes on the chair and take off those slippers with a growing sense of joy in my heart—because I'm a sinner who is loved *beyond belief*—then the grace of this week will fill my spirit with peace.

For the Journey: Learning God's Ways

This week, we celebrate God's mercy for us and our world. Those of you who are parents or grandparents or uncles or aunts have had the exciting experience of encouraging the very young to begin walking. You get wonderfully thrilled when they take that first step and then find yourself laughing when the little one goes boom.

The little one might want to cry and look to you for your response. Your smile, your outreaching hands, your gentle touch, is the beginning of his or her rising.

What would happen if your disappointment and anger at the child's failure were to show on your face and in your gestures? The child's image of self would be quite negative, and the getting up again would be slower, if at all.

God's mercy is more than forgiveness; it is also about raising us up that we might continue learning how to walk in God's ways. Mercy is not merely a judicial action, a court decision. God's mercy is a relational gesture that flows from the very center of God's creative and sustaining love for us.

When Jesus is moved with compassion for a person or the crowds, the meaning is not so much pity or even forgiveness. Jesus is pictured as being moved from deep down in his stomach, where the emotions were thought to reside. Jesus is moved to reach out, teach, feed, and lead his lost and fallen fellow humans.

Praying this week is meant to free us from the fear that God is judicially angry or disappointed with our having fallen more than once. We are invited to receive God's gentle touch and God's encouragement to rise and continue learning what it is to be God's disciple.

Mercy is above all of God's works, and we pray in the experience of letting Jesus be Jesus: "the one who saves."

So we begin this week celebrating our holiness, which involves the truth of our needing mercy, of being embraced by the truth of God's faithful upraising love. This mercy, this compassion, if received gratefully, will ultimately free us for the more important faith walk into God's future and our own. Pray gently, Jesus came to save us not to solve us.

In These or Similar Words . . .

Dear Lord,

It makes no sense. How is it that I can look back over my sins, my failings, and my faults and still be so aware of your love for me? Don't you ever get tired because I so often fail to love you and others as you would want?

But there it is: the love and the mercy. I have this image of the prodigal son trudging up the road, reciting his apology, nervous and anxious and looking up to see his father running down the road with his arms held wide. What strikes me is the joy in the father as he runs toward his son. I sense your joy in me as you welcome me and take me into your arms. I can tell that you have been out on the road every night waiting and waiting for my return with such vast love in your heart.

That's a wonderful feeling! I know I started by saying it made no sense but that's only because I'm trying to think of you loving in the same limited way I love. The photo touches me because it is such a human face of love and emotion. I see the warm, loving mother holding her daughter so tightly and I think of you, dear God and the depth of your love for me. Thank you so much for the depth of your love. It is so all-encompassing and I can take joy in it, relish it, and feel its comforting and secure warmth and strength.

Help me to carry this love throughout my week. Help me to really believe this love and not to listen to the voice inside me that tells me I'm no good and not worthy of your love.

Let me sit in silence with this love. Let me feel it enter into me, warm me. Let me receive your love, and let it surround me in your loving embrace. I am so grateful for this gift. I know I am unworthy of it and that makes it even more precious. Your love for me is so deep and vast despite the fact that you know me so well, with all of my flaws.

Thank you, Lord, for this gift of forgiveness and love. May I live this week always aware in the background of my days of your personal love for me.

Scripture Readings

John 4:5–42
John 9:1–4
John 8:3–11
Hosea 14:1–10
Luke 15:11–32

Don't be afraid.
    I have rescued you.
I have called you by name;
    now you belong to me.
To me, you are very dear,
    and I love you.
I promised to save you,
    and I kept my promise.
I am God now and forever.
No one can snatch you from me
    or stand in my way.

—Isaiah 43:1, 4, 12, 13

God's Love for Us— Healing Mercy

Guide: God's Love Heals Us

Last week we surrendered to God's forgiving embrace. We accepted and celebrated the forgiving mercy God offers us so that we might experience ourselves as *loved sinners*. This week we take the next step. Our God offers us more than forgiveness. God's love for us is so strong that it heals us.

We began with last week's loving embrace. Now we step back just like in the photo, and listen to the depth of God's love, saying,

I not only forgive you, I promise to always be with you, so you will never be alone. You no longer need your self-serving independence. I will heal your pride. I will free you from the destructive patterns that bind you. I promise to fill your heart with my love and with gifts of peace and courage and passion for sharing my love in service to others.

Throughout this week the photo can symbolize these words: "You are precious to me; I will heal you." Our journey has shown us so much brokenness. We have celebrated the forgiveness that frees us from our sins. Now, each day this week, in those background moments, we will let ourselves listen to the promise of wholeness. It is personal and addressed to me.

All week, we simply feel it. We let ourselves experience its power. Over the past several weeks, I have seen how powerless I am, how vulnerable to acting out of a rebellious spirit, to being *for myself* in too much of my life. All week I can imagine the gift of freedom from these patterns.

All week, we let our response keep rising up from deep in our hearts, "What return can I make to the Lord, for all God's goodness to me!" (Psalm 116:12) This goes beyond a feeling of gratitude and expression of thanks. A powerful experience of love always leads to a loving response. Love always leads to a desire for deeper union.

All week we will express our loving response, and our desires to be with our Lord in love. We will let it just flow from our hearts.

As always, use the resources here and online. Let's pray for one another—all of us making this retreat together—that this week will be a tender experience of the promise of healing love and a moving liberation of the response and desires from deep within us.

Some Practical Help for Getting Started This Week

This is the week when real joy and gratitude come together. Having experienced a depth of acceptance that can come only from the Lord, we now listen to the depth of the promise offered us.

When we experience the beginning of spiritual freedom, which comes with forgiveness, we are easily tempted to discouragement about how little we are able to change the deep-seated patterns of our lives. Just as I realize that I am loved and that I have a deep desire to respond in love, I also realize that there are some bad habits I need to deal with, that there are some nearly automatic ways I am accustomed to responding to temptation and pressure.

As I listen to the Lord tell me not to be afraid, I begin to realize this is not about my own self-improvement program. As I hear the Lord promise "I will always be with you," I can feel a calm come over me. The words "I will heal you" give me a hope to overcome any discouragement.

So, the first and most important practical help for this week is to keep listening to the good news that we are not alone with our need for growth and depth and spiritual freedom and maturity.

The second practical help is to take anything that is still persistently bothering me—a sin from my past, a recurring sin, a stubborn pattern of unloving, just a coolness in my heart regarding the needs of others—and ask for healing. Ask as truly as if I were driving to a doctor's office to seek a treatment. Listen to the Doctor's words, "I can heal that." Be hopeful.

Finally, throughout this week, let the response come forth from our hearts. Practice the words "What return can I make to the Lord for all God's goodness to me?"

When the joy and the sense of freedom and gratitude all come together, just rest there. At this point, our prayer is as simple as lovers gazing at each other in love.

For the Journey: Grateful Confusion at God's Mercy

Each of us can quite easily remember the worst things we have ever done. In doing so, feelings of embarrassment or shame can arise in us even after many years. "I can't believe I ever did that!" "How could I have been so stupid!" "I hope nobody else remembers my doing those things!" These are actually quite healthy interior responses to our shame-scattered pasts.

The healing of memories is not the same as erasing pictures of our more uncomfortable histories. Christian spirituality must be first of all psychologically healthy. Jesus embraced our whole humanity and lived our ways. We cannot demand or expect that God's forgiving grace ought to rearrange what is appropriately human. In short, God's grace of forgiveness, mercy, frees us for living with our memories of how we have chosen death in our pasts. Our remembering of our sins and the sins done against us does not mean we have not been forgiven or that we have not forgiven others.

This week we are invited to recall both our sinful actions and God's graceful responses. If shame and embarrassment are provoked, then how much more is our recalling of God's mercy invoked. "Where sin abounds, there does grace the more abound" (Romans 5:20).

In the Exercises Ignatius asks us to pray for "shame and confusion." He calls us to the grace of being both honest about our sins and confused about our status in God's eye. But there is another grace he asks us to request. We are to be not only embarrassed by our bad choices in the past but also confused by God's rather unjust response. Mercy is an unjust grace, and we are to stand at the foot of the cross in grateful confusion at such an inhuman response. Considering what I have done in the past and am likely to do again, here is the crucified Christ, offering me a future of his faithfulness to both my past and my days to come.

Mercy is both a forgiving and a foretelling. Each of us will return to the foot of his cross so as to live again from and with our pasts—into our futures and his. "We have here not a high priest who is unfamiliar with us" (Hebrews 4:15).

We can dwell in the shame and embarrassment of our pasts or dwell in the ongoing condition of the forgiven, who can live peacefully with our pasts as embraced by the ever-present merciful God.

In These or Similar Words . . .

Dear Lord,

How can I thank you? How can I express the joy and gratitude in my heart? It wasn't enough for you to forgive me. You now promise to be with me, with me always, with me in the healing and wholeness I so desire.

Lord, when you let me see the many complicated patterns in my life, I felt so ashamed, so embarrassed. Then you told me that that isn't the whole picture of who I am—I am a sinner who is loved by you. Now you tell me that still isn't the whole picture. I'm a loved sinner, on the path to healing, because of your faithful love for me.

How can I thank you? What can I say when you tell me you won't abandon me because I'm *unfinished*? What feelings fill me when I imagine your sticking with me in the slow, day-to-day growth of healing?

As you have been with me throughout this retreat and have freely given me what you yourself have placed in my heart to ask, I now turn to you again and beg. Please let me hear the depth of your desire to accompany me along the path to wholeness, to holiness. Please begin your healing in me. Please let your healing free me so that I can serve you as you deserve, with more and more of my heart.

Hear my humble prayer, O Lord of faithful love.

Scripture Readings

Ephesians 2:1–10
Colossians 3:9–17
Romans 5:1–11
Mark 2:1–12

The Lord then stood beside Samuel and called out
as he had done before, "Samuel! Samuel!"

"I'm listening," Samuel answered. "What do
you want me to do?"

—1 Samuel 3:10

The Invitation of Love— Please Be with Me

Guide: The Call of Our Baptism

Imagine that someone we love has just returned from a week of retreat in the Dominican Republic. Consider this invitation that he or she might make to me.

The experience changed my life, dear. My heart is filled with this image of a little girl in the children's hospital in Santiago. I feel a profound call to go there and serve for a year. If we can work out all the details to get time off here, will you please come and be with me? I know we can make a difference together. I need your love, your support. I need you. It won't always be easy, but we will have each other to lean on. And I know we can't even imagine how much more in love we will be, sharing this service together. Please be with me.

All week of this retreat, we will ponder the power of this imaginative invitation from someone we love. What impact would it have on me? If this is someone I love, would my worry about the possible hardship of the service hold me back?

And all week we will compare this invitation to the one we receive from Jesus.

Over the past several weeks, it has been the delight I've longed for—to show you how much I love you. How I have wanted you to know how much I have desired to free your heart. And now that you have asked me what you can do—what return you could make for such love—I feel eager to invite you to be with me.

Please be with me in the mission I have from my Father. *"Because God has chosen me to tell the good news to the poor, to announce freedom for prisoners, to give sight to the blind, to free everyone who suffers."*

And I need you. I need your support and your free heart. It won't always be easy. But we will be together every time you are with me in loving. If you are with me in the struggle of love, we will grow together in love in ways I can ask you only to imagine. If you are with me in the dying to self-love that is our mission, then you will be with me in the fullness of life, forever. God's reign is at hand. Together we can bring it closer. Please be with me.

Just consider this invitation all week. Feel it. It is the call of our baptism into Jesus. It isn't imaginary. It is very real. How special we are to receive such an invitation of love!

As always, make use of the helps in this book and online. And consider sharing the graces you are receiving.

Some Practical Help for Getting Started This Week

This week's consideration is about *love's invitation*. Over the past several weeks we have seen the transforming power of love. As *loved sinners* we have experienced two powerful movements: God's love for us and our desire to respond to this love. In these exercises we have grown in a sense that our relationship with God is truly a *relationship*. Everything in our faith life changes as we grow more deeply into this relationship. Whereas before I might have tried to do good and avoid evil out of a sense of obligation, I now am looking for a way to respond in gratitude to someone who has loved me at the very time I'd been an unfaithful, unreliable friend.

That's why the first part of this consideration is about an invitation of love as we might experience it with someone we love. Each of us may add a consideration that is rooted in a concrete loving situation we are in now. It doesn't have to be an imaginative one. Perhaps my spouse and I are changing and have fallen into some ruts that haven't been good for our relationship. We decide to make some major changes in the way we live our lives, for the sake of the relationship. Whatever the invitation of love is, it will have the same components: *it won't be easy, but we will have each other.*

Then when we consider the call of Jesus we can *sense* and *feel* the call in the context of the invitation of love in this relationship—my relationship with Jesus. Several of the readings we had a few weeks ago contain elements of this kind of call. When Jesus got into Peter's boat to preach (Luke 5:1–11), Jesus invited Peter into deeper water and showed Peter his power to net fish. Peter was humbled and wanted to run away. Jesus could *then* make the invitation of love—he could use a humble Peter. The woman at Simon the Pharisee's dinner party (Luke 7:36–50) shows us so much about love's power to transform us. Jesus tells his host that the difference between loving little and loving a lot has to do with how much we've been forgiven. This woman's awareness of her sinfulness has carved out in her a greater capacity to love.

Radically following Jesus can only be a response of the heart. We can all admit that too often in the past we have been too busy to even *hear* the call, let alone respond to it. Now that we have been touched by the forgiving and healing love of Jesus, now that our hearts are desirous of expressing our gratitude, we can hear the call as love's invitation.

Without jumping to our response yet, let's listen this week. We want to be *touched* by the invitation, to experience what it does within our hearts. Perhaps we will want to write out the invitation we are hearing from the Lord. Perhaps we would be willing to share some grace we have received so that the whole group making this retreat can share in it. Perhaps we want to use our bodies to pray this week. I can sit in my chair for a bit and just listen to the call deep in my heart. I can rest my open hands, palms up, on my lap as a gesture of openness and gratitude. This simple ritual gesture, or any other I might choose, then becomes an *expression* to give a lasting symbolic life to my prayer.

Finally, we can all be renewed in the sense that we are on a journey. We are growing in our ability to find intimacy with God in our everyday lives—from the moment we put on our slippers to the moment we take them off at night. In all the *background* moments of consciousness, we are journeying through our life with a richer imagination and a deeper affective relationship with the One who is always faithfully with us.

For the Journey: Knowing Jesus

We have been praying these past weeks about God's creative and redemptive love. We have also been discovering exactly who it is who has loved so much, so deeply, and for so long.

When you receive a letter or note without a signature, you might be less likely to take it seriously. If you were to receive a nice gift without any signature except for a set of initials, you might be more interested about this benefactor. There is something deep inside us that wants to know more about anybody who might like us, send us cards and gifts, and might actually love us. Who are they and why are they so good to me? What do they want in return? These are the questions that end the first section of the Spiritual Exercises and flow into the second.

We have received deeply the gifts of our having been created and then re-created in the salvific love of Jesus Christ. Who is this God; who is this God-made-man come to us? He comes not anonymously, not jotting just a two-letter signature, but Jesus proclaims his name and who he is.

We pray to study Jesus' signature and to know him as gift and the gifts Jesus offers. Be very aware that each of us has resistances to Jesus' teachings, Jesus' ways, and the path of mystery to which he calls us.

As with the men and women with whom Jesus entered into deep intimacy, their questions, their fears, their excuses, their other plans, and their natural reluctance to trust all became part of their encounter and ultimate surrender to Jesus. We ourselves want to know what we are going to be asked to do. We are called to pray this week with these questions, these reluctances, these fears well in hand and heart. They are the places where he met Peter, Nicodemus, the early church, and all the saints. We pray within the truth of our truths. Jesus meets us the way he finds us, but we have to find our fears and distrusts in order to be intimately met.

Out of love we were called into life; out of love we were called from death through sin; out of love we are constantly being called into trusting what real life can be with and alongside Jesus. His call to us is a freedom from and a freedom for. The *from* we know; the *for* is the cause of our fear and the platform of our prayer. We pray for the desire to know him and his personal love for us so deeply that, with our fears before us, we can slowly let him take them away one tremor and one tremble at a time.

In These or Similar Words . . .

Dear Lord,

I am moved by so much in this week's retreat. I see the stunning face of the little girl, standing next to a huge bed in that hospital. It's a poor place, I can see that by the cracks on the wall. But what can I do with the little girl? I can't bring her home with me.

But as I continue to look at the photo, there is an invitation I feel from you. I feel so moved when I read the imaginary conversation at the beginning of the guide for the week. What if my own loved one came home from an experience like that and asked me the same thing? Would I go? Of course. It would mean so much to us and to the way we would experience our love together, in that strange and wonder-filled place.

Is that what you are asking? You want me to consider an invitation from you to go someplace I've never been? Maybe it's someplace new but, at the same time, someplace right here at home. It's different. I'm different. But you, my loving God, would be with me in it? If I got frightened, you would be there? I feel your promise not only that you will be with me but also that the love between us will grow. What a dizzying thought!

In the past weeks, I have been amazed at the depth of love I feel growing between us, Jesus. I feel your presence in my prayers, and I sometimes get self-conscious, wondering whether I'm a little crazy for imagining a deep feeling coming from you. But in the quiet of my prayer, I *know* it's real. There is a very real love that is deepening between us. It makes me feel some deeper longing for you.

Let me sit quietly with this invitation, Jesus. I feel your calling me to something, but I'm not sure what. I feel an emptiness inside that I know you can fill, a yearning for some way to draw closer to you.

Be with me, Lord, as I pray with the photo of the little girl. Stay with me as I contemplate the invitation you hold out to me. Be with me. Fill me. Let me feel your love. Thank you for this call you are sending me. Give me the patience to stay with it this week, to pray with it, and to be patient with it.

Scripture Readings

Luke 4:14–20
Mark 1:16–20
Luke 5:27–32
Luke 9:57–62
Luke 12:32–34

"Yes, Lord.
Here I am.
Yes. Yes!"

—"In These or Similar Words . . ."
for Week 11

The Invitation of Love—
Our Response

Guide: Offering Ourselves Completely

This week we consider our response to the invitation of love. Through last week's exercise, we know that the depth of our response depends on the depth of our love for the person making the invitation. When a loved one calls for our response, we say yes. Even when we know the personal cost to us will be great, we respond because love always draws us to togetherness. We want to be *with* the one we love.

This week we will let our hearts respond to the call of Jesus. We can review his call from last week's guide. It is the call to join him in the unfolding of the reign of God. It is different for each of us. We have different gifts. Different graces have been placed in our hearts. Unique crises and experiences of suffering have shaped our unique ability to be compassionate and to suffer with others. There are special aspects of the call that are addressed to each of us, according to our age and our resources and abilities to influence others. We want to hear the call as it is addressed to us individually.

For all of us, however, the invitation and opportunity to respond is the same. Of course, we will respond by saying yes. There is no real happiness in life that doesn't involve following Jesus. The question for this week is the *depth* of our response— how completely we respond. We do not know all that our *yes* will entail this year or next year or ten years from now.

So, on one level we can make an open-ended response that offers ourselves completely to *whatever* following Jesus might mean. But the graces of the past weeks' experience of the love of Jesus for us may have so moved us that we desire to really act against anything within us that is worldly or vain or self-absorbed.

We may so desire to offer ourselves completely to being with Jesus—to be outstanding, to be a sign for others—that our response is in the form of placing no barriers to our offering of ourselves. Should our Lord so choose us, we might express not only our *willingness* to be with Jesus in his poverty and his embrace of the human condition but also our *genuine desire* to enter into that same surrender of self that was his.

Let this photo of this teacher at Red Cloud Indian School represent our response to be with Jesus in being for others. Make use of the other helps this week, especially the section "In These or Similar Words . . ." Consider sharing your graces this week.

Let the words and expressions of response flow this week. There are many weeks ahead to grow in a sense of this love–imitation desire and to explore the depths of our offering. This week we simply want to consider the response we are being given the grace to offer.

Some Practical Help for Getting Started This Week

Helping someone respond to a personal invitation of love is a little like helping someone pick out a birthday or anniversary gift for a loved one. The questions might be these: How close are you to this person? What do you want the gift to say? How much do you want to spend? At this point in the retreat, the questions are these: How deeply have I been touched by God's love and mercy? How grateful am I? How deeply did I experience the call of Jesus? What response is forming in my heart?

The first advice for this week is to get started with the simplest of responses. Just say yes. Practice saying it out loud. What does it feel like to say it in different ways? With different degrees of conviction?

The next exercise might be to be more *specific* about the *yes*. I can say yes and mean that I will accompany Jesus in the mission he has from God by being faithful to whatever comes my way *today*.

I may sense that there is a *special* kind of fidelity that is wrapped up in the invitation of Jesus to me. So, I might make my *yes* even more *explicit*: "Yes, I will be with you in the costly fidelity of loving my spouse" (or in loving my children, in accepting the difficult challenges of my job, in forgiving that relative or neighbor, or in acting against that self-defeating bad habit I have).

I may feel the invitation reaching to the areas where I have heard the call but have not responded. I might make my yes more open ended. "Yes, I want to be with you in the ways you are loving, and I will open my heart more completely to the needs of others, especially the poor" (or make time to get more involved, or respond to that invitation to service at my church, or write that letter to my political representative).

There may be such a desire growing in my heart to respond in growing love to the love of Jesus that I may want to express my *yes* more affectively. I may want to try words and expressions that are personal and loving and full of tenderness, from deep inside. I could try to express my desire to be so close to Jesus that I want to experience the same vulnerabilities he experienced and experiences today. As lovers do, I may want to place my heart with his. I can practice saying out loud, or writing out, my growing desire to know and enter into the same struggles and poverty and surrender that fill the heart of the One I love. Then, my *yes* and my desire for intimate togetherness come together.

In the weeks ahead, we will take up our desire to grow in knowledge of, intimacy with, and togetherness in service with Jesus. This week, we have the luxury of letting our consciousness be on all the ways we can say the *yes* of grateful love.

As we do each week, let the graces we are asking for be part of the background from the moment I awake, through all the in between times, to the time I prepare to sleep. I can practice taking a slow, deep breath as I go from one thing to another, as I answer the phone, as I get in the car, as I do whatever I'm doing. That deep breath can be a slow, deep *yes*. Practice letting my response fill the *background* of my everyday life and experience the power that growing in this relationship of love can have.

For the Journey: Entering Christ's Kingdom

The RSVP contained in many invitations implies that a response is expected. Upon receiving such invitations, we consider whether we have the time to attend, whether we want to go there—and for some, there is no question: of course we wouldn't think of missing it.

"Respond, if you please" is implied within the many gifts and interruptions by which God calls to us. *Response* is different from *reaction*. A response is a result of pondering, weighing, evaluating what is being asked, what is in it for us, and what it will cost. A reaction is more impulsive and immediate.

Once a year, the Catholic Church celebrates the feast of Christ the King. He comes as a servant king and a summoning king, inviting all to follow him in service of those whom he is calling, "the whole world."

We are invited by St. Ignatius to consider the many ways we have been called in our lives to enter more deeply into Christ's kingdom. In creating us, God has invested us with gifts and talents of all kinds. The Call of the King in the Exercises asks for a response to him by a response to those very gifts. Christ asked the fishermen to be fishers of souls; he asks us according to the unique and particular people we are. "I'll call you to do this, because I have given you this and that." Christ's call then is a reinforcing, a blessing, of the gift that each of us is.

We pray also this week with the melody and words of the folk song "Follow me." "Where I go, what I do and who I know, . . . take my hand and say you'll follow me."

Jesus asks that we follow him, but he will be with us and work through us and not ask anything of us that he has not asked of himself. He invites us to his victory but also to his real human way of gaining that victory.

We are asked to consider, to ponder, to reflect on the cost— what's in it for us—and to listen to the gentle invitation to the use of the person and gifts God has given each of us.

Remember, we can never totally, irrevocably surrender everything of our lives and person to God. Peter, the first of the great fishermen, left everything to follow Jesus and spent the next three years taking it back little by little. At times we would like to place it all at his feet. He will take whatever little bit of our heart, gifts, and life we can offer at any one time.

In These or Similar Words . . .

Dear Lord,

I feel your invitation so deeply. I sit with it quietly, and I recognize the longing for something unanswered in my life and realize that your gentle invitation is the answer.

I know. I feel you calling me, inviting me, offering to fill the empty longing I so often try to ignore. The emptiness that is hidden so deeply inside of me is where you belong, loving God, where I belong with you.

How is it that this invitation from you is so personal to me and so clearly addressed to me? Of course, my answer to you is yes. How can it not be, after the faithfulness and love you have shown to me in my life?

I don't know where my *yes* will take me. Your invitation is gentle, not the fear-filled one I fretted over. You are somehow asking me to change the focus of my life and, in doing that, to be more of myself than I am now. I get a little afraid when I wonder where this will take me and how this could change my life. But somehow, I know if I answer, I will become more of what you created me to be. I will become more my real, authentic self.

I am beginning to understand, my Lord, that it isn't the results of my *yes* that are important. It is my *yes*. It is the deep desire I have to be with you, to follow you, and to serve you in any way you present to me.

I long to have the real desire to surrender myself so completely to this *yes* and to you. Help me, Lord, not to hold back in my *yes*. Let me cling to your hand, not to my fears.

"For all that has been, Thanks. For all that is to be, Yes."

Yes, Lord. Here I am. Yes. YES!

Scripture Readings

Isaiah 6:1–8
Psalm 116
Luke 10:1–9; 17–21
John 21:15–19

God loved the people of this world so much that he gave his only Son, so that everyone who has faith in him will have eternal life and never really die.

—John 3:16

God's Compassion
Missions Jesus

Guide: With Jesus in His Mission

We have responded to the invitation of Jesus, the one who loves us. At some level we have expressed our desire to *be with* Jesus in his mission from God. Now we give ourselves over to the desires of this growing love-companionship relationship.

As we grow in love for someone—especially someone who has done so much for us—we experience a powerful desire not only to be *with* the one we love but also to know everything we can *about* that person. In the fascination of love we say that we can't get enough of the one we love.

For this week, and for the weeks ahead, our one desire is to come to know as much as we can about Jesus. Of course, this is not *head knowledge*. It's more the kind of discovery that leads to deeper feelings of intimacy and love, and deeper desires to be with him in his mission. *To know him more intimately that I might love him more deeply, that I might follow him more closely.*

In the early days of this retreat, we looked at our own story, through the imaginative exercise of looking through

the images in the *photo album* of our life. Now we ask Jesus to
show us *his* photo album. In our desire to know more about
him, we ask Jesus to show us *everything*—to tell us his story—
that we might fall more deeply in love with the one we will
come to know so intimately. The one who has invited us to be
with him in his mission.

This week we start at the beginning. We imagine that in
God's eternity, the Trinity of Persons in God looked down on
human history and was filled with infinite compassion that
missioned Jesus to save us. The incredible photo of Sarajevo,
Bosnia and Herzegovina, can help us imagine the span of
human history that evoked God's compassion. We know
that that expression of love by God resulted in our salvation
history—the preparation, the promises, the expectation, and
finally the birth of Jesus and his life, death, and resurrection
for us.

Let's use the helps this week to enter into the mystery of
the Incarnation, the choice of God to redeem our world. We've
reviewed all that sin and rebellion in our world has meant,
including our personal sin. Now we imagine the response of
God to the sin of the world—the missioning of Jesus. And let's
begin to express our desire to know his origins that we might
fall more deeply in love with him and be united with his mission, however he should choose to invite us to join him.

Some Practical Help
for Getting Started This Week

In everyday life, falling in love doesn't need much practical
help for getting started. It seems to just happen. Falling in love
seems easy. Upon reflection, however, falling in love does have
some elements we can learn from in our desires for the weeks
ahead. And, as we all know, sustaining a loving relationship
that leads to self-sacrificing love takes a lot of fidelity.

Think about the experience of falling in love. What allows
it to happen? What do we *do* in the earliest stages of falling

in love? Doesn't it *begin* with something we call a *connection*? Perhaps it's a connection with a total stranger. Something happens in our hearts that lifts our spirits. At the center of the *attraction* is a discovery of a *togetherness* in some way. We *connect*. From then on, the growing attraction is fed by a growing, sometimes insatiable desire to be *with* the one we love. Growing love feeds the desire for growing union—a desire for ways to be with the other in deeper and deeper ways. In the very beginning this may be quite unconscious, but before very long, we know we are in love. We start *acting on* that love. We think about, or daydream about, the other while doing all kinds of things. We call the other person more frequently and arrange to spend time together. We remember and replay our conversations. In the beginning, we talk about everything and anything. Nothing about the other person is boring. We want to know about all of the other's life experiences and choices, the other's likes and dislikes, and what makes the other the person he or she is. And at each new discovery, there is a deeper bonding. We look for ways to *express* our love, through tender words, through acts of caring, by going out of our way to help the other. Each expression deepens the love. We always remember the very first gestures of love. And the more the love grows, the more it will lead to some level of commitment—some need to guarantee that the loved one will always be in my life and some commitment to a self-giving offering of myself to the relationship.

If this fits your experience of falling in love in some way, or if it recalls what your experience was, then it will help in a practical way for the weeks ahead. We are in the process of falling in love with Jesus. We can let ourselves *feel* the growing attraction based on a connectedness. We can let ourselves *experience* our growing desire to be with Jesus—to ask questions, to express tender words, to spend more time together.

All this is practical help because it is not just an *intellectual exercise* to ask Jesus to show us his photo album. This is a matter of the heart. By this time in the retreat, we are already deeply connected with Jesus. We now desire to let our relationship go deeper.

The first pages of Jesus' photo album take us back to the beginning and show us an imaginative scene of the community of the Trinity looking forward through human history and experiencing what we can call only heart-wrenching compassion.

Imagining God's compassion to send Jesus to our world, to our lives, can be a moving experience. Keep with it. The more we imagine the Sarajevo scenes into which God's compassion in Jesus reaches, the more we understand who Jesus is. Jesus is *for us* to a depth beyond our imagining. Jesus enters into our fleshness. Completely. Such vulnerability! In no aspect of my life am I ever alone.

Throughout this week, practice saying these words: *"Lord, help me to know you completely that I may love you more intimately, so that I may be with you more completely."* Or you may want to sing the *Godspell* adaptation of these words of St. Ignatius: "Oh, dear Lord, three things I pray: to see thee more clearly; love thee more dearly; follow thee more nearly—day by day."

Each evening, before going to bed, for even a brief moment, I can ask what I ought to say to God, to Jesus. And, of course, I can feel and enjoy the inner delight of love growing and the attraction to more.

For the Journey: God's Gestures

The power of attraction begins with our watching the gestures of another person. People reveal themselves with every physical movement of hands, face, legs, and the entire body itself. People are telling others about themselves without even knowing it, simply by how they walk or carry their purse or books. The more we are physical, the more we are available to being known. Through gestures, then, we move from mystery into history. When we are invited in the Spiritual Exercises to contemplate the life of Jesus, we are urged to watch God move into our history by the physical actions or gestures of the God-made-man, Jesus.

God had made many attempts to attract our attention and response through the covenants with our Jewish ancestors. They were gestures that began, and continued through the centuries, this courtship with the human family. We now watch the increase of intensity with which Jesus comes calling. If suspicion needs distance, then our calculating selves need to allow him to perform his drama of gestures before our eyes and hearts. If prejudice needs the ignorance that distance provides, then we allow Jesus to properly inform our minds and wills so as to be in his troop.

In These or Similar Words . . .

Dear Lord,

What is it like for you to look at the world you created? You see the beauty, the nature, people caring for each other, children being born. But there is the other side. I can't imagine how much evil you see. Children going hungry, dying in their mother's arms; weapons becoming more important than the people they were designed to protect; tired and lonely people wandering the streets, not only without a place to stay but also without dignity and respect.

From the comfort of my own safe and warm home, I look into the photo for this week. The bombed-out houses, the smoke rising, the small flowers left on the tree. It suddenly changes from yet another photo of a war zone to a real neighborhood. From these houses, people went to work, celebrated family events, talked about upcoming weddings and books, borrowed flour from their neighbors. Now it's gone, a smoky rubble.

How do you look down on such a world, where we are destroying one another's homes, pouring chemicals into the waters, and valuing money and possessions more than each other? You must feel such great sadness inside. Your creations have forgotten you.

But in an incomprehensible act of love, your compassion moves you to give yourself so completely to the world you created. You express your love for us in a most unusual way— you become one of us. How could you love us that much? Knowing that it means pain and struggle and death?

Oh, Lord, teach me to love more. I beg you, please let me see and feel how you lived your life on earth. I want to know you even better and want to be with you in this world. I want to accept your invitation, to say yes to you. Now please let me become friends with you as you walk the earth. Let me learn from you, talk with you. Let me see how I can pattern my life after yours.

I am in awe at your love for us—for me. I don't have the words to express any of it except a paltry "thank you," which sounds so inadequate. Take my hand, Lord. Talk to me. Show me your photo album and your life. Help me to say yes every day.

Scripture Readings

Ephesians 1:3–14
Colossians 1:9–22
John 1:1–18

Don't be afraid.
　　I have rescued you.
I have called you by name;
　　now you belong to me.
When you cross deep rivers,
I will be with you,
　　and you won't drown.
When you walk through fire,
you won't be burned
　　or scorched by the flames.
To me, you are very dear,
　　and I love you.

　　　　　　　　—Isaiah 43:1–2, 4

God Prepares the Way

Guide: The Promise

The early pages of Jesus' photo album show us God's patient and faithful preparation to send Jesus among us. We find the photo of God calling Abram and Sarai to leave their homeland to begin a new journey. There are the births of Isaac and Jacob/Israel. The album has page after page of photos of the long slavery in Egypt, of Moses's birth and life, the Exodus and liberation, the forty years of wandering in the desert, and the early years in the Promised Land. From desert nomads to a people with a covenant: *you be my people and I will be your God*.

God sent judges to adjudicate differences between the people and then God appointed kings to rule them and then prophets to challenge them and their corrupt kings. As with any family photo album, we are puzzled and perhaps shocked to see the incredible infidelity of the people, the division of the nation, and its demise in the Babylonian captivity. Then there is the rebuilding of the temple and those final years of occupation and relative peace that came with Rome's occupation.

There is an *Advent* feel to this week of the retreat. In our growing desire to know, love, and be with Jesus, we are taken back to the years of anticipation. There's the *promise* of a land, of a king, of an everlasting kingdom. The prophets speak of what it will be like when "the day of the Lord" comes. This all tells us so much about the mission of Jesus. It will help us understand the confused expectations he will face, the rejection he will encounter, the paradoxical way he will fulfill those promises.

This week we let our minds and hearts listen to the story that prepared the way for Jesus to enter into our world and our lives. As lovers, we want to know everything about Jesus. Looking through all those early photos, we appreciate, perhaps as never before, God's fidelity and the enormous mission that Jesus was born to take up.

Throughout the background times this week, we reflect on whatever comes to our hearts. How much more do we understand who he is? How is our love growing? What do we feel drawn to express to the one who is showing us his incredible photo album?

Some Practical Help for Getting Started This Week

One of the realities we have been more sensitive to over the past decades is the importance of our backgrounds, who we are. Lots of factors go into shaping who we are today, but the influence our ancestors had on us is very important. What we are doing this week is getting in touch with the ancestry of Jesus.

This is not an intellectual exercise. We don't have to be Scripture scholars to do this. It's really very simple. And our desire is clear. We've been loved by Jesus. We want to know Jesus more completely. We will spend a good number of weeks ahead going through the Gospels to get close to Jesus in the stories of what he did on earth. This week will give us a taste of who he is and the context he came into.

Throughout this week—in all the background moments we can find—we try to stay in a *sense* that Jesus' ancestry was *Jewish*. The way he thought about himself, the way he thought about God, the images that filled his consciousness, and the culture that shaped his identity were steeped in the Hebrew tradition.

Jesus' whole sense of reality was shaped by his sense that God called Abraham from his homeland and promised him a new home. Jesus' sense of trust in God was supported by the memory that God was faithful to promise after promise. Sarah's age was not an obstacle. Pharaoh's army didn't matter. The temple could be destroyed, but God would build it up again. When I want to really know Jesus, I need to really know the faith tradition that gave him such confidence in his mission.

It's more important just to think about what we already know about that Jewish tradition than to do a lot of reading. Read the stories from the Old Testament if that helps to refresh and give *color* to the memories.

Perhaps this week, at a time when I'm walking or driving from one place to another, perhaps frustrated or angry or feeling alone, I might turn to Jesus and ask, "How did your background prepare you for situations like this, Jesus?" The answers will be the bonding graces of this week. This interior dialogue between Jesus' story and my story will be rich in helping us know him, grow in love for him, and be moved more deeply to be with him in his mission.

Use the other resources of this week. Stay faithful to the pattern of reflecting on the material for this week, as soon as I put on my slippers or robe in the morning. Near the end of each day, find some moment to express some gratitude. Consider sharing any grace received with the others making this retreat.

For the Journey: Experiencing Simple Longing

Seasons change. This globe has been rocking and rolling in a come-here, go-away relationship with its source of energy and life.

As a human family, we have also had an approach-avoidance relationship with our source of light and life. At times of our human history we have wanted God very close to protect and nourish and assist us. At other times we have struggled for our collective independence and self-direction from that confining Power. Isaiah prayed humbly, "We have become like those over whom You never ruled, like those who are not called by Your name" (Isaiah 63:19).

This week we are invited to experience simple longing. We join the yearning cold world for warmth and light. We join the ancient ache of Israel for God's love and compassionate companionship. We unite ourselves with all men and women who have struggled to be god and have gratefully surrendered to their blessed reality of being children of the one God who may go by many names but remains faithful to those who seek.

This week our prayer can be influenced by our taking the opportunities to wait with which life presents us—at stoplights, checkout counters, airports, and waiting for special people to come home soon. There are empty and hollow places in our hearts and lives. We pray with them and stay with them, not filling them up so as to take our prayer away. We are learning to ache with the world and its ancient longing for return and unity with its loving Creator. This week we go to prayer, not to escape longing, but to embrace it. There must be room in our inn and a longing in our hearts if this Advent is not to be a frenetic disappointment. We listen to the ancient sighing, "How long, O Lord." We listen to our own sighing, "Come, Lord Jesus." As the sun changes its distance from the earth each day, we join the earth in this mystery of light in the midst of darkness.

In These or Similar Words . . .

Dear Jesus,

What a different kind of week! I've never thought of the Old Testament as your own family history, but it is the stories of all of the people who came before you, who had such a powerful influence on you. When I started this retreat, I showed you the photo album of my life, the high and low points, and I saw that you were always there with me. Now, as I feel closer and closer to you, I want to see your history, your stories. You are someone I love, and I want to hear the stories that shaped you.

There is so much expectation in these stories. So many ways your people have waited for you, patiently or impatiently, over the centuries. They were looking for a king, one who would come and rule them and save them. But you were such a different kind of king! They waited for glitz and glamour, and you showed them poverty and service.

Could you feel their disappointment? You knew so well the stories that had been there for centuries, about the king who would come. Was it hard for you to be so different from what they thought? I know it's so human to want to please others. Did you struggle at all with what you were, what you wanted to teach them?

Oh, Jesus. Thank you so much for loving us all, for loving me, so much that you chose this life on earth. I can only imagine your struggles to really get across your message to people who might have been disappointed. What kind of king were you? You weren't what they had been led to expect. But you stayed and you stayed faithful to your message.

Thank you for sharing your stories, your family. Please be with me this week as I carry a sense of your history with me, those wonderful and vivid Old Testament stories, and as I see that they are really the story of waiting for you, of you fulfilling the promise to us.

My dear friend, thank you for staying with me, even when I disappoint, when I am not all that I was created to be. Thank you for your utter faithfulness and love for me.

Scripture Readings

Genesis 12:1–7
Genesis 18:1–15
Genesis 37:1–36
Exodus 2:1–25
Exodus 15:1–18
Psalm 81

Mary said, "I am the Lord's servant!
Let it happen as you have said."

—Luke 1:38

God Announces the Way; Servants Are Open

Guide: The Faith That Formed Jesus

When we look at a friend's photo album, some of the most intriguing pictures are the ones of our friend's grandparents and parents. We stare into those faces not only to look for some resemblance but also to discern something of the character, the traits, the personality of our friend.

This week, we will use the first chapters of the Gospels of Matthew and Luke in pursuit of our growing desire to know Jesus more completely, that we might grow in love with him more intimately, because we want to follow him more freely.

Our method this week will be to stare into the faces of Zechariah and Elizabeth, Joseph and Mary, and look for what they tell us about our friend Jesus. We will try to enter into these scenes in the midst of our busy, everyday lives. We will try to learn about the character and personality of Jesus by studying the faith that formed him.

This type of prayer takes some practice, but anyone can do it, because it's what we most naturally do when we meet the parents of a friend. And when we learn something about our friend's family, we learn something about our friend. For practical help in praying with these scenes, be sure to read the practical helps for prayer.

Zechariah couldn't imagine how God could overcome Elizabeth's old age. And he could not speak at all until he could say his new son's name, "God is faithful." The angel announced to Mary that "nothing is impossible with God." Elizabeth says, "Blessed is she who trusted that the Lord's words to her would be fulfilled." Mary's whole being proclaims the greatness of God and her words echo the faith of her ancestors.

As we walk around in our busy lives this week, these wonderful stories will shape our week. There will be a Zechariah-in-doubt moment, when we can't imagine God's presence, and another Zechariah moment when we can say, "God is faithful." There will be times when this week's photo on our computer screen will remind us of a feeling of being overwhelmed and saying, "How can this be?" And there will be times when it will remind us of Mary's words, "I am the Lord's servant! Let it happen as you have said."

Some Practical Help for Getting Started This Week

When directing someone through his or her desires to know, love, and follow Jesus, Ignatius of Loyola would teach them to contemplate the scenes in the Gospels with great focus and freedom. We will learn to do this, in a way adapted for our busy everyday lives, during this week and the weeks to come.

If we just read a Gospel story, we might imagine it with very vivid imagination, but that is not much different than someone telling us very vividly about a story in his or her life. That would be very special, but there is an even deeper approach, which is possible because the Scriptures are the word of God. These stories are an alive and active revelation. When we read them, something keeps happening in our hearts. The revelation continues *beyond* the text of the story.

Ignatius encourages us to *enter* the story. He wants us not only to hear the story and get the facts of what happened. He wants me to *experience* the story and let its *meaning* and *revelation to me* happen in my heart. This takes great focus and freedom, and it takes me *beyond* the details of the particular text, and it lets the story come alive and address *me* as I become a *participant* in the scene. Let's take two examples.

A Prayer Period to Contemplate a Gospel Scene

If I have the time, in just thirty to forty-five minutes, I can have a wonderful experience of almost any Gospel scene. I would begin by placing myself in the presence of God. Then, I would formally ask for the grace I desire from God during this time of prayer. Here, it might be to ask for the grace to grow in understanding of who Jesus is that I might grow in my love for him and my desire to be with him.

Then I would read the text of the story and put the text down. I will begin by slowly picturing the scene as completely as I can. Where is it? Notice all the things in and around the scene. Who's there? What is everyone wearing? How hot or cold is it there? What smells come to me? I then enter the scene even more, by becoming a character in the scene. I might just let myself be a member of the crowd, or I might become one of the principal characters in the story. When I get there, then I let the story happen and go wherever it goes. Inside the scene, the words and actions are not merely a videotaped replay of the text. Inside the scene, I can back up and fill in how the scene began, I can let what is revealed to me be played out in the words and gestures of the participants, and I can speak or simply experience my own reactions. The details of the text cease to be important as the experience of the story moves my heart. Finally, I would end with a prayer, speaking to Our Lord, heart to heart, friend to friend, in whatever way comes to me, expressing my gratitude for the graces I had just received.

Contemplating Such a Scene in Everyday Life

With focus and freedom, it is possible to let a story from Scripture become fruitful in the midst of my busy day. During this week, for example, I will wake up, and while I'm getting ready for the day (shaving, showering, putting on my makeup, getting dressed), I will think of the scenes we are contemplating this week. During this week, it will be Joseph, Zechariah, Elizabeth, and Mary. Then I will recall what the basic messages of these readings are. Here it will be messages such as these: the struggle to believe that nothing is impossible for God, the experience of having to trust God and live in faith, the experience of God being faithful. Then I will recall what I am facing today. With an open heart, some *congruence*, some *connection*, will occur to me.

It might be that there are tensions in my marriage and it is a struggle for me to believe God's faithfulness to us is stronger than our stubbornness. In this example, when I'm with my spouse, I can literally walk around in the scenes involving Zechariah and Mary—at some times really experiencing that I can't speak until I can say, "God is faithful," or at other times, "I am your servant, Lord." Or hearing Elizabeth say, "The Lord has blessed you because you believed he would keep his promises."

Perhaps all I anticipate is another routine, busy day, full of stresses that I handle in the ordinary way I do—which I discovered weeks ago in this retreat are sometimes part of the pattern of my sinfulness and the mystery of God's love for me. This week could be very rich if I walk around, in my own life's scenes, as Elizabeth. Imagine these questions, in the background, as I walk around: "It's been like this too long, to imagine any change"; "Who am I to think I will ever be more fruitful than I am?"; "In the middle of *this stuff* can I possibly imagine giving birth to a voice crying in the desert, 'Prepare the way of the Lord'?"

Perhaps the entry into a scene in my everyday life is simply memorizing a line from the Gospel story and letting it enter my heart as I say it at various *in-between* times, dozens of times each day. Imagine if, this week, we kept saying Mary's words, "With all my heart, I praise the Lord" or "God cares for me, his humble servant."

Finally, it would be wonderful if you would consider sharing some of these contemplations, the methods you used, or the graces you received. You may do this by visiting the *A Place to Share* link on the Guide page of the online retreat.

For the Journey: Praying with Imagination

"The world is charged with the grandeur of God." The Jesuit priest and poet Gerard Manley Hopkins shouts this double-meaning proclamation in the first line of his great poem about our God-loved world.

The earth is charged as with electric impulses to reveal God's glory. The earth is also charged as one might be commanded to do a certain task of importance. Both these meanings become focused this week with our considering the charge given to Elizabeth, Mary, and a man named Joseph.

It takes a certain humility to be surprised, a humility that allows there to be the unexpected, the unusual, and the frightening. This kind of humility we can call "openness" as well. It is a spirit or interior attitude or disposition that makes one available to whatever might be spoken or offered. It is not something that one can turn on or off; it is an abiding outlook or sensitivity to what is out there or in here.

We are praying with and for the grace of that humility this week as we watch and listen to three characters living their roles in the drama of salvation. It is the opening scene of the last act. We will be getting to know the ways of Jesus, the main character, by first watching those who play their parts by bringing him on stage.

Ignatius encourages those making the Exercises to try to get into the scene by use of their imagination. We use memory and our power to think and somewhat downplay this natural faculty that we all have, our imaginations. We can more easily come to truth, we think, by logic, use of facts, and use of our memories. We say that fantasy is the result of imagining, and what good is that?

Psychology uses our sense of sight to move our imaginations in what are known as projective tests. You may have taken the Rorschach, for example. In that test, you see an ink-blot and, by your verbal responses, some important truths are revealed to the person conducting the test. The person taking the test has revealed something true by using the imagination. It is more powerful than most of us believe. Ignatius trusted all the human faculties to be powers by which God could get to us.

So this week, we put this faculty to work so as to be open to the graces of openness, humility, and trust. Be attentive to where you are standing when Mary is visited by an angel. Be aware of what you imagine the angel is saying and what Mary is thinking. What do you say and do as you accompany Mary to the house of Elizabeth? What is Joseph doing after he awakens from a dream in which he understands that he must marry his betrothed even though she is with child, which he knows is not his?

Then Ignatius asks us to make reflections on ourselves and draw some insight and grace. Perhaps we watch Mary from a distance. That is good. Now we pray with those feelings of distance. Perhaps the distance comes from not wanting to have anything to do with mystery and having to trust. There we are then, praying with a truth, whose realness has been revealed in a new and dramatic way. For Ignatius, getting close to Jesus and his close friends is a way of getting closer to ourselves. This is in no way self-preoccupying or narcissistic. The closer I get to myself and my real truth, the more intimately will I find Jesus being with me. God's Truth, made flesh, enters the lives of these three persons by charging them with trust and charging them with the mystery of giving in to surprise and adventure. This is a frightening, yet consoling, week for us who watch and listen to the human struggle to let God into our private and personal scenes. We also pray to receive the grandeur of God's charge.

In These or Similar Words . . .

Dear Jesus,

Thank you for again showing me the photo album of your family. It's a little different, praying this way, and I can feel myself being self-conscious. Be with me in this. Let me feel it bringing me closer to you.

I picture Elizabeth and Zechariah struggling to have children and finally giving up. How hard that must have been for them! Did they pull together and hold each other in their pain? How did they handle it within their marriage? Then, years later, an angel appears and tells them they will have a child.

Then I look at Mary and Joseph. She was so young. I see her laughing in the kitchen, stirring up her soup by the stove, entertaining her friends with her stories. Is that where you learned to tell stories—from your mother? Then I see her— this vivacious woman with the infectious laugh—standing in an empty kitchen when the angel appears. "Will she be the mother of God?" I watch with surprise as she struggles. She knows it will turn her life upside down! Does she really want to complicate her life this way? She just wants a simple life: to cook for her friends, to marry Joseph, and to pray at the synagogue each week. Yes, she wants to live her life for you, God, but does it have to be so hard?

It never occurred to me that Mary would struggle with this. I thought she just smiled beatifically and the decision was over. But I watch her struggle with her fears and pray to

God as she always does when she is afraid. Her fears melt. Of course, if this is what God wants for her, she will do it. And there she is, still standing in the kitchen, the soup still bubbling on the stove. She looks calmly and directly at the angel and says, "Yes."

I wonder at the power of this kind of prayer before you, Jesus. I watch as your mother becomes a real person to me. I watch her say yes. Then I feel myself getting self-conscious about my own prayer. Maybe my imagination is running away. Then I do the same thing Mary does. I'm getting afraid and so I pray to God. Slowly the fear subsides.

I'm not sure I ever saw your mother as a real, live person before, Jesus. I see her say yes and I wonder about the yes in my own life. I want to know you better and to make my life more like yours. I want to be open to the messages you send, even if your messengers aren't wearing wings and halos but are the people I see every day in my life. Dear Jesus, help me to recognize the messenger. Help me to listen to the message. Most of all, help me to say yes.

Scripture Readings

Luke 1:5–25, 57–66
Luke 1:26–38
Luke 1:39–56
Luke 1:67–79
Matthew 1:18–24

So the Lord's promise came true,
just as the prophet had said,
"A virgin will have a baby boy,
and he will be called Immanuel,"
which means "God is with us."

—Matthew 1:22

We Experience His Birth, for Us

Guide: The Grace of His Birth

Many mothers, on their children's birthdays each year, tell them the details of the day they were born. Year after year, the details are repeated. At this point in our retreat, we will let Jesus show us the details of his birth. We will go beyond the words of the accounts in Matthew and Luke. We will enter more deeply than our imaginative recollection of nativity scenes. This week, we will receive the grace to experience the birth of Jesus and to understand its meaning for us.

Our desire continues. It is important for us to renew it this week. We desire to know who Jesus is much more deeply. In our observing and understanding him, we desire to fall in love with him more completely. With our love for him growing, we grow in our desire to be with him in his mission.

We will let the background of our entire week be filled with the images of his birth. They tell us who he is. As we've experienced before, this is not an intellectual exercise. It's experiential. We need to move among the scenes to know the anxiety of his parents, the poverty of their situation, the simple but extraordinary joy of Jesus' very human birth, the wonder of his being visited by shepherds, and the danger that already surrounded his life.

This week, can I let every anxiety I am feeling become connected with the anxiety of Mary and Joseph? Can I get in touch though experiences I have this week with Mary's labor and giving birth, struggling to surrender myself to give life to others? Can I come to know *the beds of hay* I am being asked to lie in? And then feel them transformed as I stare at Jesus lying there in that bed of hay? Are there poor or simple or handicapped or struggling people in my life who can remind me why the shepherds were so joyful at his coming?

The helps offer very practical entries into the graces of this week. And please consider sharing the graces you are receiving on the *Place to Share* page of the online retreat.

May Jesus, who entered our lives so humanly and completely, continue to help us to grow in a knowledge and love of him today.

Some Practical Help for Getting Started This Week

Contemplating the birth of Jesus can be a wonderful experience. And doing this in everyday life can be very powerful. Last week's helps included some basic advice for contemplating a Scripture passage in prayer period and in an everyday-life context.

We're all very familiar with the Christmas story, and we have images of the nativity scenes. This week, let's enter more deeply into the story by entering into the reality of the birth of Jesus and what it says about who Jesus is.

Each morning, when I put on my slippers or robe, I can recall what it is I wish to fill the *background* of my day. In the first few days of the week, I can let the stage be set. In the middle of the week, I can witness the birth itself. Later in the week, I can spend time with Mary, Joseph, the child, and the shepherds. Perhaps over the weekend, I can review the story through Matthew's eyes and the tyranny of Herod and the visit of the wise men and the flight into Egypt.

If we take time for prayer periods this week, it will be possible to imaginatively enter the scenes.

I could, for example, imagine being a young friend of Mary and Joseph. I could visit them frequently during Mary's pregnancy and delight in watching her sing the psalms to her child, who is listening in the womb. I listen to the faith-filled conversation of Mary and Joseph, and I watch Mary rub her stomach, as if to comfort the child with their faith. I can experience my own joy as Mary invites me to touch her belly and feel the child's developing movements. I can even take the time to tell Mary and Joseph my gratitude for their openness and their "yes." I can tell them how grateful I am for their son and for this privilege to enter into and witness the very beginning of his life. I can tell them anything I want to about my life and what I'm facing today. At this point in the retreat, Mary and Joseph can become great friends for my own life's journey. Perhaps I can be there when the news of the census arrives. How do they deal with their anxiety? Can I capture and remember their *exact* words to each other?

As I accompany them on the journey to Bethlehem for the census, what is that journey like? The roads, the fatigue, the fear, their conversation? Are they handling this differently than I have handled similar challenges or crises? What words of faith is the child hearing along the way from within the womb?

What is it like for them to not be able to find a place to stay? How is the child experiencing the words "No, no room for you here," "No, no welcome for you here"? Can I capture and remember their *exact* words to each other as they go from place to place? And what was it like when they had to settle for the place where the animals stayed? Imagine every detail, with every sense. Did they see the beauty of the place? Did they know how *fitting*, even perfect, it was?

How close can I get to the birth? As close as I'd like. If I've had a baby or seen a birth, I can imagine Mary welcoming my presence. What words do I offer her? As the contractions begin, what words pass between Mary and Joseph? Do they speak to the child in the womb? Can I get close enough to experience the birth and experience its meaning? Can I receive the newborn child in my arms? Warm and covered with blood, lungs screaming, arms outstretched? Can I wrap him in warm clothes and lay him on the bed of hay, in the very place where the animals feed? Can I feel, deep inside, *for me; this is for me*?

In the following days, what do we say to one another? As I imagine the arrival of the shepherds, what is the scene like? When they leave, can I image Mary and Joseph speaking to their son about how he will some day give his life to bringing good news to the poor?

If we let ourselves enter into these scenes this imaginatively, it will be easy to walk around in our busy lives with these images in our consciousness. And then everyday events will take on these powerful elements: anxiety, faith, fear, anticipation, journey, hardship, unexpected roadblocks, lack of acceptance, alternative plans, poverty, simple beauty, beds of hay as places of nourishment, simple acceptance. And all day long, I can be seeing and recognizing and connecting— carrying on a conversation, remembering words, noting my feelings.

When I go to bed each night, I can express my gratitude for what I was privileged to experience this day. I can offer my words to Jesus to say how much more I wish to be with him in his mission, for I am falling in love with him, because he is letting me see who he really is.

For the Journey: What Do You See?

"All is calm, all is bright." This week we watch and listen to another scene in the drama of "infinity dwindled to infancy," as the poet Gerard Manley Hopkins put it. All is not calm and bright as Joseph and Mary make their way to Bethlehem. All is bright but not calm in the inn where there was no room for them. All is not bright in the lowly stable where there was room for them and calm at the end of their long journey.

We are with the man Joseph who cannot do enough for his wife. We watch him fuss, building a warming fire, cleaning the manger. We hear the silent night, the animals eating and restlessly moving around. We hear in the stillness of the night, in the stillness of time, the sounds of the Timeless One taking time for us.

Where are you sitting or standing? Whom do you watch more closely? Are you attracted by a personal quality of these two humans as they marvel at this third human now lying in a place for feeding? Do you want to go outside, or closer? Does Mary say anything to you in word or gesture?

And now the calm is broken by the shepherds' coming. They have seen brightness, and their calm has been broken by angels singing a song of peace on earth. Are you moved to tell them anything about what you have seen? It is a scene of wonder and pondering. Mary sits there turning these things over in her heart. She had said yes to mystery when she trusted in a promise. She has much of mystery this night. All the questions of "What is this?" and "How come?" rumble in her soul and you might sit next to her and taste your own "yes" and "Let it be done to me."

Ignatius would have us be as real as we can be in the face of God's choosing to be as real as he can be for us. We know the story well, but each year, each time we pray, the story becomes more and more our own. This is God telling us who we are and what he thinks of us. The hard part of this contemplation is familiarity. By being calm, on this silent night, our prayer will bring us anew the brightness that the shepherds had heard: Today, a child is born who will bring peace to all the world. Peace to those who enjoy God's favor. Peace to those of goodwill. Peace, for Ignatius, is for those who will enjoy their good imaginations.

"Round yon virgin, mother and Child" we take our places and maybe we stand back a bit. We pray with the emptiness of our own stables waiting for the calm and bright to bless us.

In These or Similar Words . . .

Dear Jesus,

I think it's the smell of the hay that gets to me the most. I see myself standing in the cold outside the stable, watching through a big opening in the wall. There is little light, but somehow I can see everything.

This prayer has been a wonderful journey. This journey has been a wonderful prayer. I watched as Joseph and Mary traveled to Bethlehem. Mary had helped with many child-births at home, but there were no women with her now and she was a little afraid. She was still getting to know Joseph but she loved and trusted him. All of the sharing they had done over the past months as they talked about the pregnancy, his confusion, her unwavering faith, his unwavering faith, and his decision to stay with her—all of that had formed a strong bond between them, something much deeper than newlywed love.

Now as I pray with the scene, they are in the manger and all I can smell is the hay, wet and musty from the animals. How could you have a baby *here*, in the wet hay where animal droppings are all over?

What I really want is to go into the barn and help them. Can I? Oh, Jesus, can I let myself pray with my imagination and be unselfconscious enough just to go into the barn?

I walk in, and they both seem glad to see me. She is so welcoming and so grateful to have me there. Joseph has been busy clearing a place for her to lie down, and when a big contraction comes, I just hold her hand tightly. But the smell! Jesus, how could you have been born into such a smell! I tried to get out some fresh hay to scatter on the floor for Mary, but then suddenly she was giving birth and no one but me seemed to care about fresh hay.

And then you were born, into the smelly and wet hay, into the strong hands of Joseph. He wiped your face and cleaned out your nose and eyes and when you suddenly began to wail loudly, they both laughed. I laughed quietly too, but I didn't want to be in the way at such an intimate moment, so I tried to stay back. Oh, Jesus, my heart is so full! The birth of any child into this kind of place would be overwhelming. But *you*? It's cold, it smells, and where is a bed? Where is a blanket for you? Joseph has wrapped you tightly in his cloak, but you need more.

Then I realize how very tired Mary and Joseph are after their journey and the joy of this night of your birth. As Mary dozes holding you, she opens her eyes again. Would I hold you while she and Joseph sleep? I can't believe it! I settle quietly into the hay where I won't disturb them, and I hold you in the cloak. I look down at you, smell your baby neck, and nuzzle your cheek as I did with my own babies. I feel such a love for you and what you have done. You are coming into the world like this—in this incredible poverty in a smelly stable. You are doing this to be with us in the poor and smelly parts of our own lives.

Dear Jesus, help me to feel this tininess of you during the week ahead. Help me to sense your helplessness and to recognize my own helplessness and to surrender to it as you have. Help me to be small in this world and to be here for you, as odd as that sounds, as you are so much here to help me.

Scripture Readings

Matthew 1:18–24
Luke 2:1–21
Matthew 2:1–12
Matthew 2:13–23
Psalm 98

Pausing to Review the Graces We Have Received

Guide: Taking Stock

In the Spiritual Exercises, St. Ignatius urged directors of those making the Exercises to remind those making the retreat that it was important to "remain" where they "find fruit." These past several weeks of the retreat have offered powerful graces. This review week does not take up new material. The material for this week's reflection is the graces we have received over the past several weeks.

Following upon our experience of being loved as a sinner, we have had the grace of being invited to follow Jesus. We remember our personal response to follow him and our growing desire to know and be with this one who loves us so much. We have begun to let him tell us the story of God's plan and his life. We reflected on his own call and how God prepared for his coming throughout the story of the covenant in the Hebrew Scriptures. We entered into the story of his parents, and those around them, as he came to us by the power of the Holy Spirit. Finally, we find ourselves there in the stable as he is born for us.

This week of retreat is an invitation to remain there a while. Perhaps we have been too busy to take it all in. Perhaps we were not able to make the connection between his coming into the poverty of that stable and his coming into the poverty of our lives.

As we wake each morning this week, we will return to some grace for which we are grateful. It may be one grace all week. It may be simply making our home in that stable to be with Jesus there.

The grace we desire this week is *to be drawn more deeply into the person of Jesus.* The resources for this week will help us get started, take us deeper, and help us find words to pray.

We will let our reflections find their way into the background of our everyday lives. Whatever we face, each day this week can become part of the mysteries we have been contemplating, if we let it all in. Any human experience is the human experience Jesus came to enter into. This week we see and love that coming more deeply.

Finally, each evening this week, we give thanks for the new graces we are receiving this week. For even a few moments—perhaps as we are undressing for bed—we can experience gratitude for the movements of our day that connect us with Jesus, who has come into our world—to be one with us in our human experience and to invite us to join him in his mission.

Some Practical Help for Getting Started This Week

To get started this week, we must be clear about how different this week is from our previous weeks. This is a week to review, remain, and savor. We don't do this because we aren't interested in moving on but because we are interested in making sure we take in all that is being offered us. The analogy used here is not that of reading a good book and then pausing to read it all over again. A better analogy is this: A friend is showing me the family photo albums and is passing rather quickly over the early pages. I might slow my friend down and say, "Oh, these are wonderful. Let's take our time here. I really want to enjoy these pictures. Look at how young your mother looked. Is that the house you grew up in? Oh, my, the strength in your father's eyes. Oh, this picture just captures who you are, even as a baby."

Another way to describe what we are doing this week is to say we are praying, not with new material, but with the graces we have received these past weeks. I will take what I have been given and go into the gift more deeply, to remain there, to savor it. We do this because we know that gifts often contain further gifts within them. This week we will pick up the gifts we have received, and we will open them up to discover what more is being offered us.

We will do this deep appreciating of what we have received in the midst of our everyday busy lives. If the graces of these past weeks—call-and-response, a gifted sense of God's plan, how God becomes flesh for me—are to be gifts for my real life, then they will have meaning for and within my real life.

- I have said that I want to be with Jesus in his mission. Today I want to simply taste that choice with each and every task and choice of my day.

- I have understood how the Incarnation was God's prepared-for plan to save us. Today I want to consciously accept being in the flesh—including all its wonder and all the limits and diminishment of being a body-person. Concrete moments throughout the day will give me the opportunity to embrace who I am—with the body and identity I have inherited; with the choices I have made; with my physical condition, my health, my illness.

- I have seen and been touched by the Nativity. I have
  probably entered into this gifted contemplation of
  how Jesus became one of us, perhaps entering the
  scene, with those memories still fresh and moving.
  Today I want to walk around in my life sensing the
  tension in my culture to resist coming to, being
  in, a stablelike situation. I will notice—and in the
  background, chew over—just how much I enter
  into this world's efforts to cover over the simple, the
  naked, the poverty of human existence. Perhaps this
  week, I will consciously try to be myself, be more
  transparent. I might try to notice how a day would
  be if I tried not to impress others with things which
  are merely external, but to simply be with others
  with care.

Each day this week, I can find other ways to review, remain
with, and savor more deeply the gifts God is offering me
during this special journey to see Jesus more clearly, to love
him more dearly, and to follow him more nearly, day by day.

For the Journey: Linger a While

Ignatius would have us stay a while within the poverty and
humility of the stable. The child's birth begins a statement
about who he is. These events and the conditions around us
are important words here at the beginning of his long sentence
of love.

As we sit watching, we might consider any anxiety we
have about our being there. Presence is everything if we are
going to become familiar with his ways. What's the hurry? We
watch and listen. In our imaginations, perhaps our own loved
ones come to visit us there. What would we tell them about
the things to which we have been present? Perhaps we would

feel in prayer that we wanted our old friends to meet our new ones. Is there joy in our heart while we are walking quietly over to where Mary is holding the baby? Is there a reverent familiarity within us as we sit and talk with Joseph and our visitors?

There are ways to know facts and a different way we grow to know persons. Jesus, Mary, and Joseph are people and Ignatius would have us be a person and know personally those we meet here in the stable and all those whom we will see in the weeks to come. In the human process of becoming friends, we move through stages. It all begins with watching and listening and receiving whatever is being offered. We move to being acquaintances and then friends and then closer than that, partners or companions. These days we are available to be impressed by what we see and hear.

It is good for us to linger here and begin moving closer and closer not only to the crib and child but also to the personal reality of this earth-shaping event. What of the mysterious God is being manifested in this poor setting? The embrace of the loving God extends from the smallest cave to the largest planet. This God comes to everyone's stable if there is the emptiness there for a welcome. In a sense, after Bethlehem, there is nothing new to be seen but much to be understood. God's judgments are not our own. God's ways are higher and God's judgments of what is important are lower, and they meet in this lowly place where only the humble can see and believe.

So we sit for a while on a patch of straw and begin to admit. We admit him a little more each day into our own stables. We admit mystery and that we do not have it all figured out. We admit that we are loved in strange ways. We begin to admit that God's ways are beginning to attract us. We admit we need to stay here a little longer and watch our own spirits rise.

In These or Similar Words . . .

Dear Jesus,

I'm home. I'm gathered in this stable with you and Mary and Joseph. It's cold and smelly and I'm standing in cow manure and half wondering whether I didn't sit in some of it a while ago. And yet I feel so very quietly happy.

It seems like I usually feel like I'm not ready for you. At another time, I might have made you all wait outside before you came in, until I could sweep out the stable, get clean hay, scrape off the bottom of my shoes, and get some warm clothes for us all.

And I would want myself to be a better person. That's really what I see in the darkness of this stable, the darkness of my heart. I'm not just fretting about the surroundings, Jesus—it's *me*. Am I good enough to be in this place with you? It's only now as I look at you and your parents that I feel so deeply the love in this drafty, dark stable. Your tiny hands are still clutched in a newborn's fists, and when I hold out my finger, you grasp it tightly. My Lord and Savior is holding my hand! I am flooded with joy and tears that, at this moment, we are together in the kind of intimacy that has bonded humans since the beginning of time.

Dearest child Jesus, help me to peer beyond the dim light of this stable into the darkness of my own heart. Let me feel even more deeply that I really am at home here, in this place where my greatest accomplishment is holding my finger out for you to grasp. Help me to understand that you didn't come to be with me in any kind of unrealistic perfection but with me as I am right now, ankle deep in manure, tears streaking down my dusty face, and me joyfully smiling at your dozing parents as well as a cow and two oxen!

None of this seems to fit my well-ordered life, and yet here I am in this imperfect situation in what seems to be perfect happiness. My heart fills with so much gratitude to you, and

I look down on your face with a deep love. Thank you for all you mean in my life. Thank you for coming to me, to all of us, as we are in our own stables, standing in the darkness, wondering what comes next.

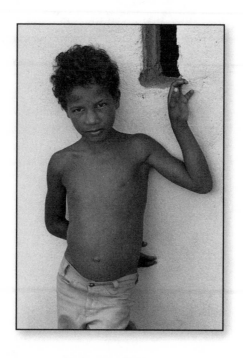

The child Jesus grew.
He became strong and wise,
and God blessed him.

—Luke 2:40

A Hidden Life for Thirty Years

Guide: The Carpenter's Son

One of the most remarkable realities about Jesus is that we know almost nothing about the first thirty years of his life. We know the stories from his public life that tell us that people who knew his relatives were fairly underwhelmed by his background. One of the charges leveled against him was "Isn't this the carpenter's son?"

This week of our retreat allows us to get to know the developing person of Jesus. Because there are so few Scripture references to the period from his birth to his baptism, we will have to imaginatively fill them in from what we do know about him.

If we reflect on the kind of adult person Jesus became, it is possible for us to reflect on what kind of childhood he had, what kind of kid he was, what kinds of issues he wrestled with, what kind of choices he made. Using what we know about the development of children, young adults, and maturing adults, we can make some wonderful guesses at some of the human issues Jesus must have faced.

Praying this way lets us get to know him more deeply that we might fall in love with him more intimately and come to our deepest desire to be with him in his mission from God.

Let us open our hearts to be shown the early childhood of Jesus. Can we go through this week imagining all the very human childhood traumas and growth that were his? And as we walk around in Jesus' teen and young-adult years, we can let him show us how he became who he is today. Can we imagine his struggles? His questions? His strengths? His weaknesses? Can we imagine his relationships at different stages of his development?

If we can get beyond what we think we don't know about those years, we can learn about how Mary and Joseph raised him. We can imagine what life in the town of Nazareth might have been like.

We know that Jesus saw himself as one called to proclaim liberty to captives and to preach the good news to the poor. We know that he saw the blessedness of being spiritually poor. We know that he understood that the reign of God was like yeast or a small seed, and that weeds and wheat must grow together. We know that he was not afraid to eat and drink with sinners and those who religious leaders avoided. We know that he saw himself as a servant, a foot washer, and as bread that would be broken and given for the life of the world. How did the carpenter's son come to all of this?

The one who loves us will show us who he is, allow us to fall more deeply in love with him than we ever imagined, and draw us to follow him more closely, day by day, week by week.

Some Practical Help for Getting Started This Week

Contemplating the hidden life of Jesus can be challenging at first. We might be frightened off by the near absence of scriptural stories to use as a base for prayer. But with a bit of imagination and freedom—and with energy from our growing fascination with Jesus—this can be a wonderful week. And doing this in everyday life can be very powerful. The last two weeks' helps included some basic advice for contemplating a Scripture passage in a prayer period and in an everyday-life context.

We might begin by an internal process of *gathering data*. What do I know about how infants develop into little children, and how children develop into teens, and how teens become young adults, and how young adults face full adulthood? We know that the stages of growth involve facing crises. We know parents are critical. We know peers are critical. We know that early choices shape the context for future choices. And we know Jesus went through all these stages of growth and development. Luke tells us, "The child Jesus grew. He became strong and wise, and God blessed him" (Luke 2:40).

Now to give *shape* to our imaginings about Jesus' growing-up years, we turn to what we know about how he turned out. We actually do this all the time. We look at someone, particularly someone we dislike or who we think didn't *turn out too well*, and we begin to make assumptions about what that person's childhood was like. Or we might meet a college-age student who is just wonderful and say that the parents must have done something right in raising him or her.

The Gospels help us tremendously in knowing who Jesus is today. The Jesus who loves me today, the Jesus I speak with in prayer, has holes in his hands. We know he's comfortable with sinners and women and others whom society of our day might be uncomfortable with. We know that he is familiar with everyday life, using images about baking bread and growing things and going to weddings and talking about how property owners manage their affairs.

Then we are ready to concretize our imagination by setting up scenes. We might begin by getting a concrete picture of what Mary and Joseph's house in Nazareth might have been like. It helps to get as detailed as possible. How many rooms are there? How big are they? What happens in each room? What's the furniture like? Where do they sleep, cook, eat, welcome visitors? Where's Joseph's carpenter's shop? What's it like? Then we might imagine the layout of the village of Nazareth. Where do children play? Where's the well? The synagogue? The market? The wedding hall? The cemetery?

Now we are ready to imagine ordinary life events that surely happened in the life of Jesus. As we imagine them and walk around in those scenes and let ourselves become a character in those scenes, experiencing and learning about Jesus, we let our Lord reveal whatever he wants to reveal to us. We can imagine any ordinary life crisis, developmental crossroad, key situation in which we develop character, or any genuine human interaction. We picture what happens, what people say, what we experience in that scene ourselves. The beauty of this kind of contemplation is that the details don't have to be *historically* accurate. The context provides an environment and an entry point for us to be open to meeting Jesus.

Some scenes we might want to develop and contemplate: very early moments as Mary and Joseph learn to care for Jesus, feed him, change him; their teaching him to talk, to walk; their having to train him, correct him, discipline him; meal scenes, playtimes, prayer time; Jesus learning to read; their taking him to his first wedding, his first funeral; Jesus beginning to help in the carpenter's shop; his emerging peer relationships with young guys, the crises faced there; Jesus' first adolescent encounters with young women, the crises he faced there; how the family faced typical problems with relatives or neighbors; Jesus as a carpenter's apprentice, his delivering furniture, his building a home; the family's dealing with the aging, illness, and death of Joseph.

At first it seemed there would be *nothing there* to contemplate, that it was indeed a *hidden* life. Now we see there is so much to learn about Jesus. None of us will have time for it all, certainly not in one week, but entering into Jesus' life somewhere and letting him reveal something about himself will be grace filled. This is quite possible in our busy lives, particularly as our curiosity and fascination for Jesus grow.

This week, let's let this whole experience of the life of Jesus, and the kind of person his life shaped, fill our imagination. We will see how throughout the week, in all the background moments, we can let ourselves become very prayerful with these delightful imaginative exercises. Our ordinary crises will help us keep his life human and real for us, and they will draw us more and more closely to him.

For the Journey: Closer to Jesus

We begin this week by looking at and listening to the events of the early days of Jesus' life. Shepherds and kings, the poor and the rich, have come to see he who has come to help us see ourselves. The Word has been spoken in the City of David, and that Word is being prepared for the hearing of all, Jew and Gentiles, near and far, rich and poor.

Joseph, who was told in a dream to take Mary as his wife, now in a dream is told to take Mary and their child away to a distant land. We are asked to consider the trust that it took for him to believe in those dreams and the faith that it took to hear them as invitations rather than demands. Journeying, not knowing to where or what for, seems to be an early theme in this historical drama. The shepherds have returned glorifying God; the kings have gone back pondering what they have seen. Mary, Joseph, and this mysterious bundle are left alone to leave for Egypt and to there wait for further instructions, which will come in time and in faith.

We are invited to visit the temple twelve years later, when the holy trinity of Joseph, Mary, and Jesus journey again to Jerusalem. This time they leave without Jesus, and fear seizes the parents. Here, Ignatius asks us to listen and to imagine their feelings. They find Jesus seemingly unconcerned about the feelings of his parents. Jesus has completed the law of being obedient to his parents and now is fulfilling a new law of obedience to his heavenly Father. He had to be about his Father's business, which will be his business for the rest of his days: speaking and doing the words of God.

We watch carefully the confusion of feelings in the hearts of Mary and Joseph. The exclamation "Why!" changes to the very good question "Why?" Mary will ask this question many times in her life. We assume that she prayed so that her questions resolved into acts of faith and hope even standing at the foot of his cross. The drama seems to drag a little bit after they all return to their home in Nazareth. For the next eighteen years of very valuable time, Jesus does something. Does he study the Scriptures of his Jewish tradition? Does he help Joseph in the carpenter shop? Does he learn, as we all do, about the human ways of loving and hating, of helping and rejecting? We are meant just to watch and ponder, as his mother must have, at the ways of God in dealing with us. It is all a mystery to her and to Jesus as well. He is preparing by being faithful to time and in time learning trust in his heavenly Father.

This week, we let amazement, confusion, and questioning be places from which to watch the beginning of the life of Christ. We pray with our own reactions of questioning and even doubting. As Jesus becomes more real to us, we ourselves become more real in the simplicity and mystery of our own lives. We are beginning to let him get closer to us individually and globally. The Word has been spoken first in the City of David and now for all and everywhere around the globe of God.

In These or Similar Words . . .

Dear Jesus,

Somehow I have always thought of you as fully formed. Yes, you were a baby, but then the Gospels suddenly have you leaving home as an adult. But what about all of those years in between? What happened when you left the stable in Bethlehem and your parents took you home?

I want to know more about the kind of child you were. Were you ever a "terrible two" as a toddler? I've never seen it written anywhere, but it is comforting for me to think of you as a delightful two-year-old, exploring, getting into things, climbing where you shouldn't in the house, getting underfoot in Joseph's carpenter shop, playing on the floor in Mary's kitchen. I like to see you like that, because it makes you so very human and it's how you and all of us learned about things and developed our curiosities about life and others with us in it.

How did you learn to read? Did Mary take you on her lap and begin to teach you the Scriptures? Did Joseph take you with the men to the synagogue? What kind of playmates did you have? What did you learn about the world by watching the traders at the market, the neighbors, Joseph's customers, and your relatives?

Joseph was such a strong influence on you, and you often stood next to him as he traded with merchants. He was gentle and trusting but strong. He even went to the market for the widow next door because the merchants always tried to cheat her. You watched as Joseph talked with them, insisting on fairness but never trying to get more than he was due.

With your engaging personality, you were a leader among the boys in your neighborhood, racing them through the town and then dashing back in laughter to Joseph's shop. Once you cheated in a race and Mary saw you do it. She took you aside and quietly told you a story, a parable, about cheating, and you burned with regret. Her gentle correction was all you needed to return to the boys with a deeper sense of honesty and of your responsibility as a leader among them.

At twelve years old you had a favorite trip into Jerusalem with a huge crowd of family and friends from Nazareth. When you got there you peeked into the temple and were mesmerized by the discussion going on there. You wanted to stay and watch, but your friends pulled at your sleeve and soon you were off, racing through the streets of Jerusalem. I know you were excited about the huge market, with its foreign wares for sale, near the temple. You looked with such interest at the different kinds of people in this big city—so different from your small town.

But in a quiet moment you slipped away from your friends, drawn back to the temple by the power of what you heard discussed there. But, Jesus, didn't you think about your parents? Sometimes I wonder about you at the temple. After all, you were a smart twelve-year-old. Shouldn't you have paid more attention than that? Mary and Joseph must have been sick when they realized you weren't with them on the journey back. But they were so relieved when they found you. As I picture the scene, Jesus, when you got home, they grounded you for a week.

But you were a wonderful child, and their discipline, love, faith, and sense of justice helped to shape you as much as Mary's story telling and Joseph's carpentry did.

I feel closer to you when I pray with all of this, as I see you slowly maturing into the adult I want to know more. When did you begin to feel that you had a special role to play? When did you sense that you were called by God in a special way? How did you begin to be a servant for others, a foot washer?

Dear Jesus, help me to understand you more so I can be more like you. Help me to find how I can serve God as you did. I want to be with you in this world and to be serving, like you.

Scripture Readings

Luke 2:22–38
Luke 2:39–40
Luke 2:41–52
Hebrews 1:1–2

God blesses those people who depend only on him.
They belong to the kingdom of heaven!

—Matthew 5:3

Two Ways of Desiring

Guide: What Do We Want?

We have begun to contemplate the life of Jesus. We have seen how, from the very beginning, his life was shaped by profound trust in God, surrender to God's plan, and the acceptance of poverty and rejection. We have been praying to know, love, and be with him more deeply. Before we move on to contemplate his active ministry, we will take a few weeks to prepare for how this retreat will shape our lives and the choices we will make as we draw more closely to Jesus.

It is desire that leads to choice. To understand the choices we make, and to prepare to make new ones, we must understand our desires and prepare to reform them.

Throughout this week, in all the in-between times, especially in the busiest and most pressured moments, we will try to understand the way of desiring that places us with Jesus. And to freely respond to Jesus' way, we will try to understand the very opposite way of desiring, a way that surrounds us in our culture today.

The clearest message from our society today, and the values that shape the advertising that tries to seduce us, is that we will be happier if we *have more*. It's subtle but consistent.

If *some* is good, then *more* is better. It seems so natural to work hard to earn more so that I can have more. We acquire and consume and become addicted to some bad things, but normally we just adopt a lifestyle that fits what we can afford. And it's not just *things* that we accumulate. We experience a desire to gather *accomplishments* or *attractive relationships*—other indications of our success. What is closely associated with this movement is the inevitable connection between what we possess and *our identity*. It's tempting to think that we *are* more, because we *have* more. We judge one another by these *measures of success*. And while there is nothing inherently bad about having things or achievements, or with the recognition and adulation that goes with them, they can seductively lead to pride, arrogance, and independence from God. *Riches, leading to honors. Honors, leading to pride.* This is a pattern of desiring we want to understand insofar as it is at work in us.

We've already seen that the way Jesus desires is quite different. His way of making choices is formed by a pattern of desiring that we've already been attracted to and that we want to understand more deeply this week. Jesus attracts us to the fundamental desire of trusting in God. When we place our lives in God's hands, as Jesus did, we experience the vulnerability of that surrender. When all is gift, we can no longer measure ourselves by what we've accumulated. This poverty of spirit, and the freedom that comes with it, often feels wonderful. Jesus, however, wants us to understand that it is quite countercultural. If riches lead to honors, poverty of any kind inevitably leads to *dishonor*. Much of our society doesn't respect simple trust in God. From the desire for spiritual poverty comes the free openness to actual poverty, if it should come to us. The less we desire to acquire, the less we will be well regarded by others. Therefore, the desire to trust in God alone leads to the incredible desire for the dishonor, humiliation, and contempt that will place me with Jesus. For, ultimately, this is the path to humility and humble readiness for any service with him. *Spiritual poverty leading to humiliation. Humiliation leading to humility.* This week we want to understand this way of desiring.

The helps that follow will assist us in entering into these reflections more deeply. They will help us get started and to turn these reflections into prayer. The photo of the land mine victims can help us reflect upon those who are on the margins of society.

Some Practical Help for Getting Started This Week

Meditating on the two ways of desiring this week is really simpler than it first may seem. It isn't about making a choice between independence from God and union with Jesus. We've already made that choice. All we are asking for this week is the grace to become aware of the ways of desiring that are at work around us. Our Christian faith tradition has long pictured this struggle as a battle being waged for our very souls. Our effort this week is to understand the movements at work in this spiritual warfare. There are these two competing *strategies* for attracting our hearts and shaping our desiring, and therefore the choices we ultimately make. The grace of spiritual freedom that is being offered us is based on the wisdom that comes from this insight into these underlying movements.

All we have to do this week is reflect on the two ways. I might keep repeating in my head, no matter what I'm doing or where I'm going, *Riches, honors, pride. Poverty, dishonor, humility.*

Eventually, I'll find ways to *flesh it out* as I keep rolling it around in my head and let it interact with my daily experiences: *Having more leads to thinking I am more, which leads to pride. Being spiritually or actually poor leads to being perceived as being less, which leads to humility.*

My desire to really understand these dynamics is fed by my growing desire to know, love, and serve Jesus. It is almost exhilarating to see clearly how Jesus, who loves me and is attracting me to himself, is *liberating me* with these insights and with a growing desire to be *with him* in the patterns of his life.

If we are faithful to this reflection all week, we will see how these movements are at work in our everyday life. We will also experience the *taste* of a desire to reach for the freedom being offered us here.

As our devotion grows, we might use a very simple exercise to dramatize the seriousness of our desire and the depth of our sincerity. It's as if we say to ourselves, "I really *do* want these graces."

We might first turn to Mary, Jesus' dear mother, whom we spent time imagining these past weeks. We can ask her to beg her son, on our behalf, to give us these graces. We can name them. We can say we want to understand these ways of desiring and to be given spiritual poverty, and even actual poverty, if that would help us serve God more and help us save our souls. If it helps, our prayer to Mary could end with the Hail Mary.

Then we might turn to Jesus and ask him to beg his God and Father, on our behalf, for the same graces. And if it helps, our prayer to Jesus could end with the Soul of Christ.

Finally, we might turn to our God and beg on our own behalf for these graces. And our prayer to God could end with the Lord's Prayer.

We remember that our progress is by God's gift. And one gift opens the way for our receiving another. We have seen how these graces prepare us for new graces. All we need to do is stay open and trusting that the One who brought us this far along our journey will graciously remain faithful in bringing us to its conclusion.

For the Journey: Who Are We?

When Jesus is baptized, he publicly assumes his position or mission as the Beloved. We contemplate this scene and wonder whether we want to go with him. He is heading for his temptation by the devil to not be obedient to what he has heard. He remains faithful to his baptismal dignity and destiny. Throughout his life he will hear other calls and identities that will call him away from being the Savior.

At this point in the retreat we consider how we answer the universal human question, "How do I know who I am?" Our identities are fragile enough, and we wonder about and we hear various invitations to just how to answer this most important question. This is a week of considering and evaluating the strategies of the two main contestants in the battle for our souls' identities. There is the Evil One and his minions in one army and there is Jesus peacefully inviting us.

We pray this week to understand how positively attractive the plan of the Evil One is to answer the question about our identity. First the Evil Spirit will attract us to solve the question by accumulating possessions that we will be able to point to and say, "There! I must be somebody, because I have all these material trophies."

So we pray about how attracted we can be by those things that in themselves might be very good. Do we possess them or do they possess us? The rich young man was tied up by what he had, because those things told him and others who he was.

The next step the enemy of our human nature tries, after we still cannot peacefully answer the question by the amount of our goods, is to attain a position of importance by which we have other people telling us who we are. Prestige and power are so attractive, and the Evil One tempts Jesus and us as well to define ourselves by our titles and honors. The advance is toward greater and greater dependency on something outside ourselves to create a sense of worth and self. The third and most fatal trap of the Leader of Destruction is a radical stance of independence from God, a prideful appreciation of ourselves as our own cause and sustainer. We need not God but more things and people as testimonies to our undaunted spirit.

We turn then to the camp of Jesus and he who has heard from his Father exactly who he is, who invites us to listen to that same baptizing and confirming voice telling us that we too are the beloved of God. We have listened to the Tempter and his offerings; we spend time considering how attractive the invitation is to so believe who we are that we need not solve the question by having something outside us affirm ourselves—a spirit of simple openness, which Jesus called poverty of spirit. We know what things are, what they are for, and where they have come from.

We hear the freedom from and freedom for expressed when Jesus invites us to not be concerned about being humbled or even humiliated because our names and identities are given to us by the Creator.

Freedom from possessions and prestige allows us to walk the walk of the free Jesus, whose actions and style we are contemplating this week. He knew who he was and simply asks us these days to so accept ourselves as the beloved of God that imitating him becomes our way of expressing who we are. We live now not merely as our independent selves; Christ lives in and through us.

This week we face our own ways of being attracted by the tricks and trade of the Seducer. We also find our hearts and minds being drawn to the ways and wisdom of Jesus.

In These or Similar Words . . .

Dear Mary,

I haven't spent a lot of time talking with you since I was a child. Now, doing this retreat, I want to move closer to your son, and I find myself wanting to get to know you. In the past weeks as I've been praying, I have been picturing your life and the way you lived it with Joseph and Jesus. I see the way you taught Jesus, and as I watch you struggle with being a parent and dealing with married life, I find myself able to connect with you more.

I want so deeply to receive the grace and courage to live my life the way Jesus did. Please ask Jesus to accept me in my struggle to serve him. I can see the many ways I cling to my pride, arrogance, and independence from God. I always think of independence as a very good thing, and yet when I try to be independent from God, it's really my way of trying to be God. Go to your son, please, Mary. Ask Jesus to help me to accept my limitations, to embrace them as sources of grace in my life. My struggle for perfection won't bring me closer to God, but my struggle to accept my flaws might.

Hail Mary, full of grace . . .

Oh, Jesus,

I turn to you in such humility. I am so drawn to the kind of life you led on earth, but it seems impossible for me! I am so caught up in the subtlest kind of struggle: a few honors or awards here or there are nice, but they're never enough. I want more honors, more recognition. I have restructured my life to fit the opinion of the world, and slowly I have drifted away from the kind of life I want to lead.

I ask myself, What can it hurt? At first it's just some applause, some people telling me how wonderful I am. But then I read the retreat guide for this week and I know what is wrong—how subtly the world has changed my viewpoint. Suddenly I am the honors and awards, and if they stop, what will become of me? I have lost myself in this career-climbing, out-of-balance life. It's not that my job is bad or even that the honors are harmful; it's that I have lost my perspective. Dear Jesus, ask God to help me to resist the things in this world that keep me from the humility and poverty of a life like yours.

Jesus, may all that is in you flow into me . . .

Loving God,

You put your son on this earth to become one of us—for us. Help me to watch how he lived and pattern my life after his. I know that with my arrogance and independence I want to do this myself, but now, at least for today, at this moment, I know I can't. Please, God, give me the grace to imitate Jesus in all things, even those that frighten me. I'm not even looking at the dramatic things like torture and crucifixion, but at the way he simply put the needs of other people ahead of his own. Dear God, I want to live like that but I am sometimes so far away from it.

Be with me in my struggle. Let me only seek your approval for my life. Let me become aware of the quiet ways in which I am seduced away from following your son to becoming a slave to the world.

Our Father, who art in heaven . . .

Scripture Readings

Matthew 5:1–16
Galatians 5:16–26
Philippians 4:11–15
1 Timothy 6:6–10, 17–19
1 Peter 5:1–11

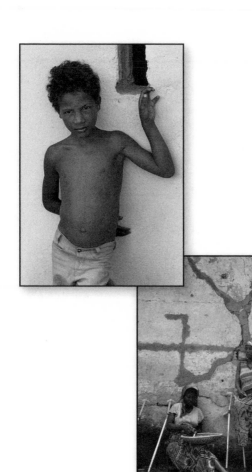

Pausing to Review the Graces We Have Received

Guide: The Graces Take Us Deeper

We pause again to let the graces we have received penetrate our hearts more deeply. We are making this retreat in the midst of our everyday lives. We let these reflections become everyday for us—more familiar and comfortable. We *prepare* to move into the contemplations that Jesus will show us about his own life's journey.

This week doesn't take us into new territory. It just takes us deeper. We begin this week with our desires. I renew my desire, my passion, my choice, to be *with Jesus*—to want to *know* him more intimately, to *love* him more deeply, to *follow* him with more of my heart. This week is not one of deeper struggle or more intense thinking. This is a week of affirmation. All week, in many very concrete ways, in the background experience of the in-between times, I say, "Yes, this is what I want. This is what I choose. To be with you, Jesus."

This is a week to deepen these graces by *enjoying* them. I know that this deepening relationship with Jesus is changing me, freeing me, moving me to learn even more about him, all because I love this person who loves me so completely, so unconditionally. I just feel it all week—and enjoy it. I like the way I'm becoming. I like what is opening up in me.

All week I will pause, perhaps especially in the most difficult moments, and smile with a deepening inner smile. The riches and the honors just don't have such a hold on me. The poverty experiences, even moments of humiliation, don't terrify me as much. I smile because I understand and am becoming more and more *attracted to* Jesus' way of living his life—moving away from the path to pride and toward the path to humility before God.

Each night this week, I let my words of gratitude come from deeper and deeper in my heart. The messiness or difficulties—even the failures or sin of my day—don't take away my gratitude. They deepen it. I'm grateful because Jesus is drawing me into a joy I hadn't known before. It is a joy that is dependent not on my successes but on my life being placed with Jesus, in God's hands.

Some Practical Help for Getting Started This Week

A week of review is very different from the other weeks of this retreat. Here we are just staying where we find fruit. We are savoring and enjoying the gifts that have been given us, the way we savor and enjoy some very special time we have spent with a loved one. It stays with us for a while. Not moving on to something else too quickly really deepens the love we have in our hearts.

We use the same methods that we have been using in the weeks so far. Very brief but focused times throughout our day make this retreat happen. Perhaps this week we will pay more attention to our feelings, particularly what seems to give us deep joy, often beneath lots of conflict, and what seems deeply disturbing, often seeming to push the joy away.

The movements in our hearts help us become more attentive to how the Lord is working in us. We become more attuned to the language of God within us by paying attention to which movements seem to come from God and which seem to come from something much more base (indecent, nasty, cowardly), much more intent on our not growing. When we are moving away from the Lord, the movement from God will often be the one that disturbs us or confronts us. The base movements tend to keep us comfortable and lazy and make us come up with all kinds of excuses for why this way of living is actually good.

When we are moving toward the Lord, the way we are in this part of the retreat, we can trust that the Lord is offering us deep joy, a sense of liberation, courage, and peace. The Lord is offering us something that stirs inside of us that will be saying, "This is good. This is right. This is from me. Trust it." And when we are experiencing the desire to know Jesus, to love him, and to follow him, we can expect that there will be conflicting base desires that will raise doubts, confusion, even an unexplainable sadness. They tend to reinforce old habits, which seem to become unreasonably more powerful just now. We can chase these movements away so easily just by saying, with a smile, "I know what's going on here. I don't need this. I'm going to choose life and the peace that is being offered me. Good-bye."

The Triple Prayer

As our devotion grows, we might again use this very simple exercise to dramatize the seriousness of our desire and the depth of our sincerity. It's as if we say to ourselves, "I really do want these graces."

We might first turn to Mary, Jesus' dear mother, whom we spent time imagining these past weeks. We can ask her to beg her son, on our behalf, to give us these graces. We can name them. We can say we want to understand these ways of desiring and to be given spiritual poverty, and even actual poverty, if that would help us serve God more and help us save our souls. If it helps, our prayer to Mary could end with the Hail Mary.

Then we might turn to Jesus and ask him to beg his God and Father, on our behalf, for the same graces. And if it helps, our prayer to Jesus could end with the Soul of Christ.

Finally, we might turn to our God and beg on our own behalf for these graces. And our prayer to God could end with the Lord's Prayer.

We remember that our progress is by God's gift. And one gift opens the way for our receiving another. We have seen how these graces prepare us for new graces. All we need to do is stay open and trusting that the One who brought us this far along our journey will graciously remain faithful in bringing us to its conclusion.

For the Journey: The Human Christ

There is an old puzzle that goes, "How far does one have to go into a forest, before that person begins coming out?" In the Spiritual Exercises there is no real middle that one passes through and begins exiting. Now that we have come this far, we might have realized that there is no exiting. We are not in a trap or a maze; rather, we have entered the life process of slowly becoming aware of our need for a savior and then who this savior is for us.

This week we are called to consider the realness, the humanness, of Christ's on-going living into our life's struggles. Here is the man, born of woman, a man like us in every way, growing, maturing through his life's events to embrace our lives and their realnesses.

When was the middle of Jesus' life? Here is the mystery. Once Jesus entered his life, each of us became the center of his everlasting life. He has entered our human struggles and there is no end, so there is no point at which he begins exiting. We pray these days with the constancy, the fixed commitment of his love for our life's journey.

The basic human fear of our being abandoned, our fears of being alone, become the entering place for his being for and with us. We will watch him meet the weak, sick, poor, rejectable, contemptible, and basically sinful representatives of our fallen selves. Each of us knows how repulsive certain people can be by their selfishness, their anger, and their greed. We can pray with our feelings toward these people and with those feelings watch Jesus embrace, touch, and bless those very same kinds of people. We are beginning to pray with how his ways and our ways are so different, but with intimacy and familiarity, those ways of viewing and acting do change.

What is so hard is our being so comfortable and accustomed to what seems naturally good and right. It is not that Jesus has come to be an example; he is what life is supposed to be and he lived it as invitation.

We pray with our reluctances, our "You've got to be kidding," our own weaknesses in responding. We know our pasts, but we have grown. We fear our inadequacies in completing promises or intentions for the future. What we have is only the present and the grace to look within and around at ourselves and the world, which continues needing the unabandoning touch and embrace of Jesus.

We pray with goodwill this week and consider how radically, how differently, Jesus lived and desires to live through us. Our conversions are not moral but now more relational and attitudinal. Most of the great saints of history have had to live in the presence of their pasts. They had to face how fragile their sense of fidelity might be. They also faced what Jesus faced, the personal and faithful love of God. With God, even our conversions are not impossible. God's love is perfect, and our responses are good enough for God to bless and continue to redeem this world.

In These or Similar Words . . .

Dear Jesus,

As I review the retreat from the past few weeks, I am attracted so strongly to one thought from last week's guide: when all is gift, we can no longer measure ourselves by what we've accumulated. What surprises me, Jesus, is that the thought attracts me. I'm not frightened by it; I'm drawn to it. It sounds so different from the way I live my life, and yet there seems to be such freedom in it.

I want to embrace the poverty of spirit you are calling me to—I want to embrace this yearning I feel in my heart. That feeling is an invitation from you to join in the kind of life you live because you know I will be happier in it. You know better than anyone the emptiness I so often face when another success stares blankly back at me from a mirror. It's the kind of success that means so little, and yet it means way too much.

I want to embrace the poverty that leads to humiliation. Humiliation isn't something I ordinarily look for, but in this context I see where it is totally opposite to the honors and success, the things and riches, I often use to fill the dark and vacant spots in my heart.

I stare at the retreat photo from last week. The two women who are land-mine victims lean up against the cracked wall. What evil forces cost them their legs? How many family members have they lost in this struggle for power, greed, riches, honor? And then I see the Scripture quote below the photo: "God blesses those people who depend only on him. They belong to the kingdom of heaven!"

That, more than anything, is what I long for in my life. Please God, teach me to depend on you. Show me how to give my life away to you, for you. Guide me in the path of life you chose for yourself.

Like a New Year's resolution, I want this right now, at this moment—but can I sustain this longing? This week's "For the Journey" says it so well: "They had to face how fragile their sense of fidelity might be." Please, Jesus. I can't continue to want this on my own. I need to recognize your call in this and I don't always want to listen.

I know my faithfulness is flawed and that I don't always recognize that all is gift in my life. Please help me to understand from someplace deeper than I often want to go that this call to simpler, humbler, poorer, is the way you are leading me to happiness.

All I want is to know Christ
and the power that raised him to life.
I want to suffer and die as he did,
so that somehow I also may be raised to life.

—Philippians 3:10–11

Three Kinds of Responses

Guide: Motives

Before returning to the life of Jesus, we will take one more week to lay further foundation for our upcoming reflections. We know we will be drawn more deeply into our relationship with Jesus and that this will call us to greater freedom in the choices we will make for living our lives.

This week we will spend our background time reflecting on a simple case study. We will consider an imaginary but very real situation, to reflect on three ways of responding to it.

We consider a case in which someone finds him- or herself in a way of life or in a pattern of acting that he or she is not entirely proud of. It is important to note here that we are not talking about something really bad but something that has not been very responsive to God's movement in that person's life. It might be an attachment to the way he or she looks, or simply the amount of creature comforts that he or she has become dependent on. It might be an attachment to a pattern of always using his or her gifts to manipulate others to get his or her own way, or simply being attached to the habit of mediocrity in family life or work—getting by with as little effort as is required of me.

Having one or more of these cases in our minds all week, we will consider three kinds of responses.

1. Wanting to free oneself from this attachment and really be more attentive to God's calls in one's life but *just never getting around to doing it.* This type of responder has only good intentions but never gets around to putting them into action.

2. Wanting to free oneself from this attachment but ending up rationalizing it to such a degree that one can work out a justification that makes it seem that *this way of being attached is actually what God wants.*

3. Responding to the attachment by neither trying to keep it nor trying to get rid of it. This is a desire to free oneself of the attachment in such a way that one becomes no longer attached to it. Rather, one becomes more responsive to and more attached to however God might be moving one to act here and now. The desire becomes purer. *One wants only what will be of greater service to God.* Whatever would be of greater service becomes what motivates one's choices.

As we prepare to contemplate more of the life of Jesus, we beg for the grace this week, perhaps every morning when we rise, and each night, before we sleep. We ask for the gift to respond more and more freely, that all we choose might be for God's greater glory and the salvation of our souls.

Some Practical Help for Getting Started This Week

This week is a second very simple meditation to prepare us to continue contemplating the life of Jesus. It also helps us to be quite careful and humble in the responses we will make to God's invitation to free us more and more.

It is so important to remember that this is not about the choice to be a good person as opposed to a bad person. It is far subtler than that. We're assuming that we have great and growing desires to know, love, and serve Jesus, who has freed us from our sins.

This week is a reflection on ways of responding. As we enter more deeply into a life that is drawing us into the pattern of Jesus' own life, death, and resurrection, we are reflecting on how it is possible to avoid the freedom that is offered us. Then we are realizing that the only response we truly desire is to be free before everything in our lives.

To be human is to develop attachments to things, to habitual ways of being, to needs for security and identity. The purpose of this week is *not* to do an inventory of all the attachments in our lives. Our purpose here is to reflect on our response and to simply express our desire to be free.

Practically speaking, we can spend the whole week putting into words how we desire to respond. We can wake in the morning and go to bed at night saying the simple words, "My life is in your hands." The threefold prayer to Mary, Jesus, and God to beg for these graces of freedom can be very powerful this week.

As we encounter the attachments of our life this week, we can simply acknowledge the attachment and then ask not to be rid of it but to be *free* before it. Let's take a simple example. If I find that I'm embarrassed to admit that I'm too attached to my appearance, I can ask for the grace to desire only God's glory, and not mine. I might put into words how I long to use my appearance not to attract people to me for my own self-absorbed purposes but so that I might be better able to serve God, and save my soul, by not caring whether I look attractive or don't look attractive. My one desire will be to be *however* I can be to better serve God.

It might happen, that in the course of this week, we will struggle with this. We might discover a real resistance to being this free. We might find ourselves uncovering the *depth* of some of our attachments. We may discover a voice from inside saying, or perhaps shouting, "I don't *want* to surrender so much. I don't *want* to be spiritually poor and I sure don't want to experience *material poverty*." It's at this time that there is great power in simply asking for the grace, with the voice in my heart that *does desire* to be more and more with and like Jesus and to continue to be invited by God into that union and imitation. We can say, "Lord, I want *only* what would make me truly free and truly happy."

Finally, we can express our gratitude to God, who is drawing us closer to Jesus. We know we aren't there yet, but we can feel the attraction growing within our hearts as we express our developing desires.

For the Journey: The Freedom Jesus Offers Us

It is very good for us to remember the purpose for our going through this retreat. We are at the halfway point, and we might have lost sight of just where these various considerations and prayers are leading us.

Ignatius knows well the unfreedoms of the human condition. We have regrets, fears, resentments, ego needs, physical drives, and personal histories, all of which naturally pull us toward satisfying and protecting ourselves. Our personal wills fashion a lifestyle in which all the previously mentioned forces combine and play out in our choices of life.

The central aim of the retreat is to seek for the will of God and then desire to live God's will in our lives. Two difficulties arise in this area. We must face the strength and varying influences of our own wills and then extract ourselves from doing what we want and try to do what we hear God inviting us to do. Let me say this very simply: this doing of God's will is not easy!

Ignatius uses the natural attraction that we all have to possessions as an example of how difficult it is to let go, not just of material things themselves but also of our attraction and desires for it. The pulls on our lives of power, security, and independence are similar to the pull of gravity here on the earth. We learn to adjust to it so we don't jump from high places or expect to bounce when we fall. It all becomes quite natural to us, and we hardly ever refer to or reflect on its pulls on us.

Ignatius presents us in the Exercises with an invitation to live more aware of the gravitational pulls on our spirits and the choices that flow from within. The planet called Christ has different gravitational demands. They take getting used to and, as with the earthly forces when we are growing up, we can trip and fall trying to live these new laws of life.

We have been praying with the events of Christ's early life, and we will return to consider his public life, but Ignatius has us pause this week to ponder honestly how difficult it is to leave the natural laws of personal gravity and what it would cost to try to live more in keeping with the freedoms that Jesus offers. It is important to pray with the awareness of how of this earth we are. His call is gentle and patient but also insistent. We think we know what is good for us, and yet he offers us a second opinion as one who loves us more than we love ourselves, if we can imagine that.

This week we resist negativity about how of this earth's ways we are. We pray in hope that by his grace, little by little, we can be so attracted by Jesus and his ways that, though we can possess this or that, we become freed from anything possessing us.

In These or Similar Words . . .

Dear Mary,

A week like this is humbling when I look at the patterns in my own life and see how they are designed for my honor and glory instead of God's. It's so easy to convince myself that what I am doing is God's will when I suspect deep down that it is for my benefit.

I look at the way I distance myself from people. Mary, did you ever want to distance yourself from all of your critics or the people who wanted to judge you? I can feel myself doing that, and then I look at the three responses for this week. Often, like the first response, I'll tell myself, "Yes, I know it might not be a good thing to always pull away from people and relationships." I'll decide to change, to make myself more vulnerable and open—but somehow I never get around to it.

Or I might tell myself that there's nothing wrong with protecting myself from pain and that doing so helped me cope with a difficult childhood, so it's really OK if I simply pull back from connecting with people. After all, would God want me to expose myself to the pain that can happen if I really let people see who I am?

Mary, ask Jesus to help me. I want to do it all alone and I simply can't. Ask Jesus to help me see that if I ask for help from him, it's not a failure but an opening up of myself.

Jesus,

I need your help and I don't know where to start. I do so many things that protect me from harm and isolate me from other people. When I look at the photo of Mother Teresa this week, my first instinct is to dismiss her. "I can't be holy like that! Do I have to be like her?" But maybe that's not what you are inviting me into, Jesus. If I look at her life, she was so open to others, so vulnerable to their pain and suffering. Maybe she just reminds me that I keep myself from feeling others' pain as a way of not feeling my own.

Jesus, help me to interact with people in a less closed-off way. But maybe that's not it either. It's not about fixing me. Maybe it's not whether I protect myself but whether everything I do is for God's glory. I'm not sure what all of this means now. All I know is that I want to get to know you better and to free myself from the things in my life that keep me from living life the way you did.

Jesus, please ask God for the grace to choose only what is for God's glory and the salvation of my soul. If that means that I should open myself up more to people, then give me the help I need to do that.

Loving God,

I turn to you and beg you for help that I might be able to choose only what is for your glory and the salvation of my soul. Help me to relate to people in a way that is not for my self-protection but for your glory. Accept my humble prayer and give me the guidance and wisdom I need to live this day only for you.

Help me to remember that I can get easily confused and sidetracked in examining my own motivations. God, sometimes too much scrutiny merely makes me self-absorbed. Help me to focus only on you, on how I can serve you and how I can live out my life in the way you desire for me.

Scripture Readings

Luke 18:18–30
Luke 9:57–62
Matthew 6:24–34
Philippians 3:7–16
Psalm 131

"This is my own dear Son,
and I am pleased with him."

—Matthew 3:17

Journey from Nazareth to the River Jordan Baptism

Guide: Jesus' Journey into His Mission

We now return to contemplating the life of Jesus. We reflect on the *two ways of desiring* and *three types of responses* we have prepared to let Jesus show us his life. Our desire to know him more intimately, as we fall more deeply in love with him, is shaping our desire to be with him more completely in his mission. We have been drawn to ask more and more deeply that we might be given the graces to choose only and whatever is for the greater glory of God and the salvation of our souls.

The part of Jesus' life we focus on this week is his journey from home into his mission. At some point, perhaps around the age of thirty, Jesus leaves Nazareth and goes down to the river Jordan, where John is baptizing. He enters the water and, against John's reluctance, asks to be baptized along with everyone else. The heavens open and we hear God's affirmation of him.

The material that follows will assist in getting started with this contemplation. All week we want to walk around in this scene in our everyday life. As we imagine Jesus leaving that little house in Nazareth, we have so many questions to ask. Why did he leave? What process of reflection, of freedom, led him to go? Can we imagine the farewells? What did people say to him? What did he say to friends, to relatives, to Mary? As he walks the roads down to the river where John was baptizing others, what is he thinking? What is he desiring, choosing, longing for? With what words is he praying? As he watches John baptize humble sinners, looking into their faces as they go into and come out of the water, what is he feeling? As Jesus wades into the river, deeper and deeper, and then is immersed in it, can I imagine what is streaming through his consciousness? Does he experience his own incarnation into the depth of our humanity? Does he imagine the surrender of his own desires to God's spirit drawing him to complete emptying of himself for us? Does the picture of his being nailed to a cross to die flash before him? And when his face emerges from the water and God's voice breaks through the clouds, what exhilaration, freedom, and peace fill his heart?

As we go through this week imagining parts of these scenes over and over, in the very midst of the movements of our everyday lives, we come to know Jesus and our own desires more deeply than we could have imagined. We come to see how familiar he is with our own struggles to respond to God's call. How often this week will we leave one place we are at home for another place we know we must be? How often this week will a "yes" involve a deeper entry into a simple solidarity with all of humanity? Can some experience of my living out my own baptism this week allow me to experience deep intimacy with Jesus in his baptism?

We can end each day with a prayer of gratitude and personal conversation with Jesus, speaking our desire.

Some Practical Help
for Getting Started This Week

Getting started this week is easy. Every one of us has had some sort of experience of leaving home, of responding to a call, of having to leave something or someone behind to journey in fidelity to who we are. So letting Jesus show us his departure from Nazareth for the river Jordan will be easy, if we let our imaginations be informed by our own experience.

Try to take this first part of our week's contemplation and let it be the grace we pray for as we step out of bed each morning. Use words to help shape the day's reflection: "Lord, show me what led you to leave your home in Nazareth for your very public ministry. I so want to know you and grow in love for your way of responding to your mission. Show me what you want to show me about the journey of your heart. I want to listen today."

By the middle of the week we will be ready to contemplate the baptism. The scene is simple, but the drama is tremendous. Think about it and imagine it enough to let it have the power it can have. If we love Jesus, we have to have some feeling about watching him approach this baptism. He doesn't *need* to do this. He could say to God, "I have not sinned; I don't need to do this act of repentance. I'm not like those people entering that water." But, of course, that is not his response to God's call that he become one with us. We can allow ourselves to be caught up in feelings of awe and appreciation and joy for him as he comes to the freedom of this baptism. We can let ourselves be touched by what his baptism means for us.

Each morning we can ask for the graces we need: "Lord, let me *be there* as you enter into the waters of baptism with me and for me. You are wonderful and I love you. I so want to be with you and together with you in your mission. Give me what I need this week to surrender more and more for God's glory and the salvation of my soul."

Each evening, we can spend a brief moment speaking to our Lord in our own words. We express our gratitude. We share some image that touches us. We tell him about how some moment in our day became *different* because we were contemplating this journey of his life this week.

Whenever we feel the desire for deeper graces, we can make the triple prayer to Mary, Jesus, and God the Father, as was outlined two weeks ago. Use the prayer help "In These or

Similar Words . . ." to help with the expressions of intimate prayer that can help us own the graces of this week.

Finally, please consider sharing some of the graces that come to you as a result of these rich contemplations in everyday life.

For the Journey: Bathed in Christ

We are praying this week with two sensitive and frightening experiences in the life of Jesus and subsequently in our own lives. One is the celebration and reflection on the baptism of Jesus. In the Exercises, Ignatius would have us first watch Jesus leave his home and his mother. This scene is not in Scripture, but Ignatius cannot picture Jesus casually and callously moving out without a tender scene of separation.

Jesus will ask his own disciples to leave everything, including their father and their boats. Ignatius too had to leave his family and home and knew the tension that is caused by the call of Jesus to leave everything to follow him.

Freedom does not mean heartlessness or insensitivity. He came to enhearten us so that his joy may be complete in our joy. Is looking back allowed? Are longing and loving allowed in being companions with Jesus? As followers, we are called not to live compulsively obsessed. We are invited to be dedicated not dead-icated. We watch with reverence the tender scene of Jesus kissing his mother and perhaps lingering and looking back at his mother, whose tears begin her son's baptismal journey. She had said, "Let it be done," and now it is beginning to be done.

We are then encouraged, when it is right for each of us, to watch and listen to the ordinational baptism of Jesus. He hears who he is to his Father and has his own personal prayer and discernment blessed as well. He humbly accepts both the pouring of water by John and the proclamation that he is now publicly known to be the Anointed, the Christ.

He has received the gifts of the three kings at his birth. He has received his self-awareness in his own prayer. He now receives confirmation to be the beloved servant from his Father to his people.

We listen, we watch, and we reflect on his dignity, his destiny, and his own trust in both. Ignatius asks us to turn toward ourselves and reflect on our having been baptized into that same dignity, destiny, and—yes—awareness of whom each of us is. To be bathed in Christ is to be immersed in his being servant of God's people and confirmed as beloved of his Father.

In this one week of considerations, we move from tenderness to tremblingness because of the frightening dignity we receive by being one with him. We tremble as well when we consider our destiny as servants. We might find ourselves standing on the bank of the river of his baptism and wanting to check it out or talk it over with Jesus, who is accepting who he is while turning to us tenderly. Does he say, "Come on in; the water's fine?" Does he understand our timidity, our valid questions about his future and our own?

Jesus is baptized and begins taking his life very personally and seriously. Ignatius asks us to move in that direction as well. Jesus did not know where this would lead him; we do not know either, except we do know that he will lead us. Tender timidity is our sense of self as we begin to immerse ourselves into Christ.

In These or Similar Words . . .

Dear Jesus,

So many things touch me this week as I watch you. How did you ever leave home? I know how much your mother meant to you and that you lived with her in a home filled with great love. How did you hear the call from God for something more in your life? How did your "yes" feel inside when you prayed and knew you were being called to become one of us in such an intimate way?

I watch you leave home and walk off toward the river in the distance. It was so painful to leave home. You knew it was right, but that didn't make it easy. And what were you walking toward? Were you afraid of the uncertainty that faced you? Did you wonder exactly how this would all end up?

I see you on the riverbank watching John baptize the others. They are prayerful and deeply moved by these baptisms. At their baptisms, some of the people are quiet, and some are exhilarated. All of them have been moved to join with God in a new and deeper way. I see you watch their faces as they emerge, wet with water, shining with joy. Your love for each of them is so clear. You sit and pray for each of them with such a deep connection and love.

And then you join them.

You wade into the water where John is standing. He is surprised and resists, but only a word from you convinces him that this is right. He holds you and I watch as you are plunged into the darkness under the water. What is it like for you to be in that darkness, that coldness, eyes closed? With your birth you have joined us as part of the humanity in this world. Now with this baptism, you have joined in our sinfulness. What can that possibly mean?

Then your head comes up from the darkness in the water and I see the same joy shining on your face. You throw your head back, flinging water, and laugh out loud for pure happiness. John joins you in laughing, not knowing exactly why but knowing that he loves you. You turn and walk to the riverbank toward me and pull yourself up to sit next to me. I love to look at the joy on your face. You ask me if I want to join you in the waters.

Oh, Jesus, no. I'm too afraid. I want so much to be with you, to join you in this mission of yours. But I'm not worthy. I'm not good enough. Gently, you take my hand and talk with me about my fears. What was the phrase in "For the Journey" this week? "Tender timidity." I feel the incredible strength and dignity of your presence next to me. Just because you want so much to be near me, Jesus, I feel less afraid.

What is it, Jesus, that makes me so afraid? If I take the plunge in my life, as you have, and accept this baptism, what does it mean for my life? How will my life be turned upside down? What will I have to leave that now feels so at home? Maybe what scares me most are the questions, What if I fail? and What if God is asking me to do more than I am capable of?

Still holding my hand, you ask me whether I can feel the love God has for me, the love you have for me. Yes, I can. But the fear is still there. I'm not worthy. I look into your face and see the love and friendship you have for me. I see that I am worthy just because of your love. Maybe I always think of myself as unworthy around you because it keeps me from getting too close. If I tell myself I'm not worthy to be with you, then I avoid the invitation from you that can change (and disrupt) my life. Keeping myself at a distance from you, Jesus, means that I can't hear you as clearly.

That isn't what I want. I don't want to be distant from you anymore. Over these past weeks and months I have grown so close to you. I feel the strength of your presence and know that I want to go with you, to be with you in your life, and to have you with me in mine.

Thank you for the love and friendship you give to me. Thank you for caring so much for me.

Scripture Readings

Mark 1:9–11
Matthew 3:13–17
Luke 3:21–22
John 1:26–34
Philippians 2:1–11
Romans 6:3–11

After the devil had finished testing Jesus
in every way possible, he left him for a while.

—Luke 4:13

The Temptations in the Desert

Guide: Testing

There is no greater self-revelation than to let one's temptations show. In this week's contemplation, Jesus shows us what he wrestled with. In our growing desire to know him, in our deepening affection for him, in this powerful attraction to being with him in his mission, we are drawn to understand his struggles. As he reveals to us the depths of his inner process to be free to do God's will, we see that Jesus knows us in our growing desire to be free.

There are a number of key elements in our contemplation this week that help us frame our reflection.

- *Jesus does not run from temptation.* In fact, the Holy Spirit of God leads him to the desert to face these demons.

- *Jesus fasts first.* He wants to be lean and prepared and alert and hungry.

- *Jesus is facing his identity.* The temptations are all about how he is who he is.

- *Jesus is confronting temptations to use his personal power for himself,* rather than for others.

Freedom is all about confronting the temptation to use one's power to feed oneself. The demon is always to focus on our hungers and to fear we will starve. Self-absorption always defeats our ability to freely give ourselves for others. The Gospels tell us Jesus knew this temptation. He learned to depend on God's word for his nourishment. Then he was free to be broken and given as food for us all.

To be free, we must confront the ability we have to use our gifts to attract others to ourselves. It's a tragedy to be gifted and manipulative. Our inner self becomes hollow when we desire only attention, affirmation, to be liked, to be accepted. Jesus faced this temptation. He chose not to arrogantly use his gifts. He chose freedom. His first choice was to give himself to whatever God desired. Then he could joyfully accept unpopularity, being unattractive, and even being rejected if they helped him be who he was called to be—for others.

The desire for freedom will always bring us face-to-face with a desire for our own kingdom. What can I collect, achieve, accomplish, be recognized for, point to as a symbol of my self-worth? Jesus knew this temptation. He came to live in the freedom of the prayer: "The kingdom, the power, and the glory are yours, now and forever."

Use the helps to get started and support this week's contemplation. Throughout our week, each and every day this week, these temptations and the freedom Jesus chose can be part of our consciousness. We will grow in love for him. And our own desires to be with him in his freedom will grow.

Some Practical Help
for Getting Started This Week

Getting started this week is easy. Read Matthew's and Luke's accounts of the temptations. Then put the text of the Scripture aside. What is important for us in contemplating this mystery of Jesus' being tempted is that we enter into its meaning.

The kind of reflection that will help is to ask, What is going on when *I* am tempted? Doesn't it mean that part of me really *wants* what I'm tempted to? It doesn't matter whether it's the temptation to eat a whole bag of potato chips or of chocolate, or something much more serious. A battle is going on between *some want or desire* and the inner conviction that this is not good for me. What does it mean that, in his hunger, Jesus was tempted to turn stone into loaves of bread? This is not about a temptation to use magical powers frivolously. It must be that there is a battle between his inner desires.

All week long, in various in-between times, we can reflect on what this inner struggle to feed himself must have been. What kind of concrete, personal examples come to mind?

We may want to take some individual prayer times in our busy schedule to pray, using our imagination, to picture a scene in which we can *witness* the temptation for Jesus. I might become a character in that scene and find myself touched, moved with admiration and love, at the self-revelation with which he graces me. I could do this with each temptation.

Throughout the week, however, we can benefit from the supportive patterns we have used in the retreat from the beginning. As I get out of bed in the morning, I can focus my attention on what this week is about and what my desire is for this day: deeper insight into this person who has loved me with his very life and who I am coming to understand and love more deeply.

Throughout each day this week, I can make use of all the background times not only to reflect on the images of the tempted Jesus that come to me but also to see this mystery acted out in the mystery of my day-to-day life. If he was really tempted in every way I am, then I can learn about his heart and personality by letting the temptations that come up in my daily life give some shape and color to my reflection on his temptations. Then, every time I feel tempted to be angry or cynical, manipulative or noncooperative, dishonest or unjust, indifferent or just plain selfish, I learn about the heart of Jesus.

Finally, every evening when I go to bed, I can take a brief time to express my gratitude in words that become increasingly personal—friend to friend—expressing what I feel and asking for what I desire.

For the Journey: Walk in Faith

We pray this week with the listening Jesus. This past week, we watched his being baptized and his going public as the Christ. He heard his Father publicly announcing that he is the Beloved.

In the Gospel of Matthew, this baptism takes place at the end of the third chapter. Matthew offers us the drama of Jesus' listening to the Tempter at the beginning of the very next chapter. Ignatius presents us with the same sequence. Jesus, because he has listened to his Father's ordaining voice, is free to listen to the unordaining or discrediting temptations of the Evil One.

We enter the scene to watch and listen ourselves to the attractiveness of the devil's invitations and the simplicity of Jesus' self-acceptance. Jesus does more than reject the temptations; he more honestly receives himself. We are aware of our attractions to riches, power, and control. These are all so many ways of trying to find and express our fragile selves. Ignatius offers to those who would want to follow Jesus the experience of rejecting the falseness of any identities that come from material or social validation. Jesus has listened and believed and now begins the life of living out his belief in his Father and who he is in his Father's own words.

We pray this week watching the devil try to impeach Jesus. It is a tense debate and we are encouraged to be faithful to the tensions created by our own fragile senses of who God says we are. The Evil One constantly works to falsify our sense of our dignity, our ordination into Christ, and our holiness. We too have been baptized into Christ and his dignity. We too hear the insistent urgings to not believe in the me whom God has created and Jesus has blessed.

We perhaps listen to the sigh of relief that Jesus makes at the departure of the Tempter. Perhaps it is a prayer of gratitude and a peaceful prayer of trust that comes from his knowing who he really is. He also knows the Tempter will return in many ways during his life and that it is not the last time his baptismal ordination will be challenged. We may watch him resting there alone but not unaccompanied. He is beginning to experience the unity between him and his Father, which does not have to be proved by changing stones into bread.

Ignatius invites us in the Spiritual Exercises to walk more by faith in the care of God's love than by using signs and proofs as crutches for the journey. This pilgrimage to which we are called is not easy and extremely against the ways of our world and our own natural desires for maps, road signs, and assurances. We pray patiently with ourselves this week and watch Jesus turn knowingly toward us as he invites us to pick up our fragile lives and walk into his future and our own.

In These or Similar Words . . .

Dear Jesus,

How human you really are! Thank you for inviting me to be with you in your temptations. I was touched to be with you at such a vulnerable time. I know you were hungry after forty days without food. Yet the devil's suggestion to turn stones into bread didn't seem like a challenge to do a magic act. It seemed to be more about how you resisted the temptation to fill your immediate need to end your hunger. You wanted to end your fast only if it seemed like God's will, not a more worldly motivation.

The bigger temptation was to wrestle with the appeal to glorify yourself. The devil invited you into something that appeared not so bad: the devil promised you power and glory. What a temptation it must have been to justify yourself, to finally force people to see you as a powerful and important person.

I watched as you struggled with it, telling yourself first that it would be a good thing, that it would advance your ministry and help you reach more people. Then you had to stop and hold it up to God, your father and the source of your life. As you bowed in prayer, you knew that your glory wasn't what you wanted. You wanted to be free enough of the chains of self-absorption that your deepest desire was to serve God. You couldn't possibly accept power or honors—unless it came from God.

Dear friend, how can I learn that kind of strength from you? How many times do I fail in my temptations and make a decision based not on God's desire for me but on my own desire to avoid humiliation or to look successful? Help me to want only to serve God, to be free of the traps of accomplishments and recognition, and to feel the joy that comes with that freedom.

As I get to know you more and more, I want to be more like you, to live my life like yours. Thank you for your friendship. Thank you for being with me and for inviting me so deeply.

Scripture Readings

Mark 1:12–13
Matthew 4:1–11
Luke 4:1–13

Then he chose twelve of them to be his apostles,
so that they could be with him.

—Mark 3:14

Jesus Calls Others to Join Him

Guide: Being Drawn to Him

As Jesus reveals his story to us, we can't help becoming drawn to him. This week, we have the privilege of contemplating Jesus as the one who calls companions to service with him. If we were inclined, in the past, to view God's calls to us as obligations about which we might be ambivalent, we are not there now. In this retreat, we are growing in a sense of such attraction to the person of Jesus and his way of responding to his own call from God. We are being drawn to be with him with deep desire.

The Scripture readings this week give us the text of various *calls* that the Gospel writers present for us. Throughout this week, let them flow in and out of consciousness. Any time we can take to prayerfully imagine any of these scenes will enrich the week. We can enter into the scenes, to see and to hear, to be caught up in the drama of the call-and-response.

This week's real power is in our ability to let it be one in which we become keenly faithful, throughout each day, to a sense of Jesus' being with us in our day. As I awake, prepare for the day, go to do my work, interact with people, take breaks, experience a range of emotions, make mistakes, struggle to be zealous, find opportunities to be compassionate, make tough decisions, experience the joy of loving and being loved, and return to sleep with grateful prayer—in all of my day—I can savor the reality of Jesus calling me to *join him* in saying "yes."

We are experiencing the power of this retreat. Praying over and over for the grace *to know him more intimately, to fall in love with him more deeply, and to be drawn into the pattern of his own life more completely* does indeed transform our lives. Love changes the way we make choices because love changes what we desire. The more we fall in love with Jesus the more we love what he loves. Being with him becomes a growing desire.

Use all the helps this week. The practical helps will help name three degrees of being with Jesus. Our journey is one that will call us to rearrange the choices of our lives to allow us to be more and more with Jesus. The one who asks us, "What are you looking for?" knows our answer, and always invites us to "Come, follow me."

Some Practical Help for Getting Started This Week

It is said that imitation is the highest form of praise. That saying proves to be quite true as we progress through this retreat in our everyday lives. Having experienced the love of Jesus for us, and focusing on the details of his birth and life so far, we are asking, "Lord, help me to be with you, to imitate you, in surrender and love."

We grow in this imitation. Our desire to be with Jesus transforms our lives. There is no desire to rebel from God completely. The love we feel in our hearts casts out a great degree of our selfish desires. With our eyes fixed on Jesus, it is very unlikely that we will give in to serious sin.

Love eventually transforms the heart even more. In time, we take on the desires of the other. Not only does selfish rebellion recede from my life but also a variety of things I had naturally *preferred* become less important. Before growing in such a love for Jesus and a desire to be with him in his mission, I would have said that, given the choice, I'd prefer to be rich rather than poor, to be honored rather than dishonored, to have a long life rather than a short one. In these options, and in hundreds more in my life, *what is best for me* would have been the focus and criteria for my choice. Now that is changing. As the attraction of love grows, I want *whatever* would help me be with and like Jesus. And, of course, this kind of love lightens our spirits and makes what might have been difficult or a challenge so much easier. We become more loving and compassionate, more generous and self-sacrificing, more courageous and just, throughout our daily lives.

Love that grows always desires deeper and deeper union. It's said that older couples, who have loved each other deeply all their lives, can anticipate each other's needs—if one is sick, the other will even desire the illness rather than see the other suffer from it. Freed from our previous rebellious desires, even our previous preferred ways of choosing, the desire for complete union can grow. In love, we come to want the experience of the other. If the other I love is in poverty or suffers or is rejected, I no longer want to stand apart so as to shield myself from the experience. It becomes natural for me to see the poverty or suffering or rejection as part of our relationship. I simply *want to be with the one I love.* The more I see Jesus giving himself to whatever is for the greater glory of God and service of others, the more my desire is to fall into the hands of a loving God, just as he did. As I see the poverty of his surrender, I want it too. As I see him stripped of recognition and purified in his desires, I want that too. And as I see him surrender his very life to the will of God, I desire to be one with him there as well.

In the context of our contemplating Jesus' calling his disciples this week, we can *feel* our desire to go with him in his mission. We can ask, even beg, for a deeper degree of love to grow in us. Attraction leads to the desire to be *with*, which ultimately leads to the deep desire to be *one* with him.

We can recall these reflections as we wake each morning this week, at various background times throughout each day, and we can return thanks in the most tender of words at the end of each day. Our hearts are being prepared for the contemplations in the weeks to come.

For the Journey: Watching and Listening

We are considering these days the gestures of Jesus. Ignatius invites those making the Exercises to be so present in the events of the life of Jesus that we let those events almost happen in our own lives. We are so there that we are there watching and listening to this God-made-man coming alongside every human condition.

After being tempted by the Evil One, Jesus walked along the shore and called to two sets of fishermen. He was apparently so attractive that they left their former means of living to live lives that gave them their new meaning of life. Jesus came as light and here enlightens his first four followers. They made some initial choice to stay in the light.

As his early followers found out, staying in the light, staying enlightened, can be too brilliant, and so at times they drifted away in the shadows of doubt, resistance, and self-preoccupation. Jesus' response was always an encouraging invitation to return and reform. By his instructions and deeds of caring for his followers, Jesus gave them information about who he was and who they were. Information then leads to reformation and ultimately to conformation to the person who reverenced them enough to allow them to wander.

Jesus offered them signs or gestures that made his way of living worth a good try. This week and for the next few weeks, we are invited to see these gestures of Jesus in such a way that we might more closely consider our own reformation and conformation to his ways. He does not call to us from way up ahead, or above, but actually from beside and behind. In a strange mysterious way, we watch him in front of us, but he calls to us from behind. He so reverences our freedom that he allows us to take this road or that, and he watches and follows. So here is this Jesus who we watch so as to follow, and then he follows our choices and watches how to more lovingly offer us gestures that prove his fidelity to us.

Our prayer this week centers on our awareness of his actions in the lives of the people who were called early in the public life of Jesus. Have we seen enough of his ways to be attracted to make some adaptive changes in our lives that will make him more available for other people to see his ways in our own? As with the early followers, we are not going to be perfect in staying in the brilliance of the light of his teachings. Our moving in and out of the light is how we follow him and why he follows us reverently and compassionately. The major changes in the lives of any human being are results of having deeply met other influential and impressive people. The prayer this week is a response to the gestures of a God who wants to be influential and impressive while still respecting our free choice. Is there a choice welling up in our prayer this week?

In These or Similar Words . . .

Dear Jesus,

I hear your call to me. I feel so deeply how you love and desire me to be with you in this journey. I watch as you call the disciples lovingly and with such friendship. You teach them and send them out into the world to heal and spread your message.

As I read about how you call the fishermen on the shore, I too hear your call. I want to go with you. I follow you down the beach, and you stop and turn so gently and look at me with such love. "What do you want?" you ask me.

I stand there on the beach in my bare feet and try to articulate what I feel in my heart. I want to go with you where you are going. I want to make choices in my life that bring me closer to you and make my life more like yours. I want to take your hand and walk with you into towns, into marketplaces, even into the places in my own life that frighten me.

I feel your call to me in such a direct, personal way and I see you loving me so deeply as I try to conform my life to yours. I know I am making a decision to adapt my life, to see things with your eyes, to make choices differently. And I see you watching me with love as I make these changes.

My dear, loving friend: Thank you for calling me to be with you so closely. Thank you for wanting me with you. Thank you for giving me this deep desire to be with you. My love for you is growing with each passing week, as we become better and dearer friends and as I feel your love for me. I want to be with you in a new and deeper way. Teach me. Let me live each day realizing that you are with me always, even when I fail in my desires. Allow me to feel you leading me in front and guiding me from behind.

Stay with me, dear one. Let me feel your love. Let me say "yes" to you. Thank you for staying so close to my side.

Scripture Readings

Mark 1:16–20
Luke 5:1–11
Matthew 9:9–13
John 1:35–42
Mark 3:13–19
Luke 9:1–6
Luke 10:1–12
Luke 9:57–62
Luke 19:16–28

Pausing to Review the Graces We Have Received

A Week of Review: "He Calls Me"

As we journey in the retreat, we pause to stay awhile with the graces being offered us. Before moving ahead to hear and see Jesus and fall more deeply in love with Jesus in his life and ministry, I pause to savor what has just happened. I walk around with a deep sense of peace this week.

"He calls me." Throughout the week, I let myself experience these words more and more deeply. "He wants me. He needs me. He wants me to be with him. He invites me into his own experience of being called, of being servant. And I'm feeling that I want it very much. I want to be with him so much. There is something here that is different, that feels wonderful, that gives me new energy, a new freedom."

We remember that in this review we will not be going to take on new material. It involves pausing to let myself catch up with what has been happening in me, with what I have been given, with what I have been excited by, with what I have been saying "yes" to.

It is a simple week, with the same patterns of previous weeks. I'll continue to pause when I wake and give thanks at the end of the day. I'll still use the in-between times, the background times of my day, to refocus and be attentive to what is going on. This week, however, it becomes simpler and more peaceful. I may just pause from time to time and take a deep breath and smile as I remember some aspect of the previous weeks as it relates to what is going on in my life today. I may face something difficult, experience with more conscious awareness some part of my life's commitment, or just notice that this moment is one that is extremely ordinary and routine. If I pause and slowly breathe the word *yes*, the graces of these past weeks become renewed and deepened.

Our desire continues in the same way. In our pausing this week, we will experience how we can grow in our desire. As I appreciate the depth of the invitation offered me, the more intensely I want to move forward and let Jesus show me the rest of his life. My desire to be with him and to be like him grows the more I am attracted to him who has loved me so much.

Some Practical Help for Getting Started This Week

The most practical reminder for getting in to this week is to let it be simple. It is a part of our busy world to think that because nothing *big* and stimulating is going on, nothing is going on. That assumption leads to restlessness and an inattention to the subtle movements in our hearts.

Perhaps I need to wake each morning and pause at the side of my bed and say, "I just want to appreciate what has been given me, offered me." Those words, or any others that come from my heart, will help me focus my day around attention and gratitude. Then the subtler things that were perhaps overlooked or underappreciated can rise to the surface.

Remembering keeps graces alive. Throughout this week, look back at important moments in my ordinary life these past weeks. Review the graces that were there in a brief background experience. If there was some experience, feeling, thought, prayer, that especially stirred my heart, I can return there and enjoy it at a deeper level in a new context this week.

Being re-collected is really just a simple process of collecting what is really valuable and important, over and over. Our lives are being filled with grace these weeks as we are drawn, by love, into the life of the one who invites us to join him in his own mission.

For the Journey: Pondering His Ways

When going on a journey, we would want to have made arrangements, procured maps, made reservations. With all these things done, we might still wonder whether we are on the right highway and whether we really want to stay here or go there.

This week we are encouraged to pull off the highway to check things over before continuing this following of Jesus. There are some important questions to be answered. We might be asking Jesus some, and we might be asking ourselves some others. These questions are prayerful even if they might seem a bit doubting and distrustful. The newly called fishermen did not seem to have any questions or doubts when Jesus first called them, but as we read on in their relationship with Jesus, they had many. They did not know what lay ahead for them, but as they bumped into problems and challenges, they would turn to Jesus with puzzled faces and say things like, "Don't you care? We're sinking!"

So we pray for comfort as we review and preview. The call of the Gospels and the Spiritual Exercises is both to come and see and then to go and do. So what have we seen these past weeks of this sacred journey? What of his ways are delightful or disappointing? Perhaps when contemplating his birth, the sense of humiliating poverty was too dramatic for us.

Watching and listening to Jesus being told that he was the Beloved was a great consolation, because we are, in him, the beloved of God as well. There are some serious implications to being the beloved, and perhaps we would rather be a little removed from such intimacy.

However we find ourselves reflecting with such questions, they do provide us with a prayerful agenda. However we find ourselves, God does too and is always laboring to encourage us through our doubts to trust. "Fear not," God says to those whom God has called in the past. "Fear not," Jesus says to us. Fear not our truth, our questions, our doubts or resistance. As with the early apostles, when bumping into Jesus, we are bumping into ourselves. We can become a bit discouraged with ourselves, for after being prayerfully attentive these past weeks, we can find ourselves still burdened by the "old leaven." Jesus loves us the way he finds us, and while this can be embarrassing, it is how Jesus most encountered people, in their seemingly humiliating truth.

There is a future calling into life as well. This week we might pray with our desires to go on or the sense that this has gone far enough. We know that once Peter allowed Jesus into his boat, Peter's life was changed more than Peter could imagine. There were many who found his ways and teachings hard to hear and took other roads. Jesus invites and not demands. Jesus has love to share with all of us no matter what our responses might be. Jesus requests and not requires.

This week we pray with our usual fears of wanting to know the future, the specifications, and the success rate. The grace of God reverences what is natural to us, and so it is very important to pray simply with those fears, humbling though they may be. His teachings, his way of relating, his pattern of responding, all are a little different from our usual ways. He lived freely his identity. He works to offer us such freedom, but our ways are so familiar and his so new.

This week we pray with our own Scriptures, our own record of Jesus' actions in our lives. We will see more next week of the strangeness, yet attractiveness of his style. This week we rest with our histories of faith, doubt, listening, desires, and frailty. "The favors of the Lord are not all in the past. Every morning they are being renewed."

In These or Similar Words . . .

Dear Jesus,

I feel like I want more. More what? More of you in my life. A deeper connection. I want to spend more time with you—like I do someone I love deeply. I want to learn from you, to imitate the way you live, to listen closely to what you are asking me.

I look back on the last week, and I realize how much I am inspired by you, and how something deep within me is stirred to want to do more with my life for you. You are calling me and I feel it inside and I want to drop everything and go with you.

But even with my strongest desires, I still face the fact that I am so very human and flawed. Even in the midst of serving you this week, I recognize how the pull to riches, honor, and glory can pull me away from you. You are so grounded in poverty and humility, and yet I continue to find myself turning away from you—turning instinctively toward the honors and glory. That's not the way to find you. But this time, I don't turn away from you in shame. With you holding my hand, I look at what happened this week and I see my flaws and I know you see them too. You know me so well and you love me—even with all my imperfections.

Dear Jesus, I want to take a rest from the struggle. Let me sit at your feet and gaze up at you. I hear you and am moved. My heart is on fire as I imagine myself in your service. I know that you chose Peter as the leader of your apostles. He was a man with so much imperfection and so much heart. Please—I ask you, Lord. Lead me the way you led Peter. Befriend me and let me feel your love for me. Let me spend my days with you, learning as you teach and watching as you heal. And when I find myself distracted by the dazzle of riches and honors, let me remember how much you loved Peter and how you love me.

Jesus, I want to give my life to you. I want to follow you and be with you always. I want to love you as much as I feel your love.

I tremble in gratitude as I say thank you for wanting the same thing.

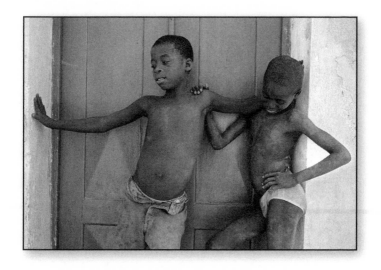

God blesses those people who depend only on him.
They belong to the kingdom of heaven!

—Matthew 5:3

Jesus Shares His Message

Guide: Let the Word Penetrate

This week we seek to know Jesus more intimately by entering into the depth of his words. Lovers listen. Lovers devour the words of the other. This week we want to come to savor the words of Jesus and let them penetrate our hearts.

When Jesus' turn comes to read in the synagogue in his hometown, he picks up the words of the prophet Isaiah, which must have been part of his prayer for years.

"The Lord's Spirit has come to me, because he has chosen me to tell the good news to the poor. The Lord has sent me to announce freedom for prisoners, to give sight to the blind, to free everyone who suffers, and to say, 'This is the year the Lord has chosen'" (Luke 4:18–19).

When Jesus begins his preaching in Matthew's Gospel, he looks out and sees the crowd that gathers to hear him. They are not the spiritually rich. They are weary and they are full of mourning. Justice is something they can only hunger and thirst for. And they are the ones reviled and rejected by self-righteous religious folks. Jesus announces to them that they are truly blessed by God.

We can't help but fall more deeply in love with Jesus as we see how his mission takes him to the heart of our life's struggle. He offers us good news and freedom. If we had expected Jesus to be saying that we have to be holy *before* we come to God, we are quite surprised when we actually chew his words. His preaching gives us such a powerful picture of God's love for us, precisely *in the midst of* our poverty and powerlessness. And his message contains the clear and all-encompassing commandment to love one another the very way God loves us.

This week, let us become familiar with the message that comes from the heart of Jesus. Read the Scripture readings this week very carefully. Commit them to memory. Imagine the scenes, the people, their lives, their reactions.

From morning until night this week, in the midst of all we do, in all those background times, we can let the words of Jesus console us. Especially in the places where I might feel captive and in need of freedom, I can feel his presence. I can become so conscious of his being with me throughout this week as I show mercy and try to be a peacemaker. I can hear his words of assurance and blessing when I feel quite spiritually poor and discover I can't depend on my strength but only on him.

Use the resources to get started. Lovers listen. As we let his words echo around in our life this week, our hearts will be drawn ever closer to his. And our desire for this union will grow this week.

Some Practical Help
for Getting Started This Week

We want to let the words of Jesus draw us to him. Who is he? He is one who stands up and says that God blesses us when we are most vulnerable and in need. He proclaims it, he lives it in his own compassion and outreach, and he died for saying it. This is who he is—the one we are coming to know and love and be drawn to follow.

We must begin by listening. We want to listen with the fascination and focus of a lover. How many times have we heard the readings selected for this week? How many times have they left very little impression on us? This week we want to go to those readings hungry for everything they can tell us about Jesus.

If it helps, read each reading many times throughout the week. Read each reading all the way through to get the context and the whole message. Then, go back and read it more carefully, noticing words that surprise you. It can help to compare translations of the readings. Notice how seeing different ways of saying the same thing can reveal the meaning more deeply.

After a particular reading is familiar, reflect on who the audience is. For whom is this good news? Who is threatened by it? Can I place myself in that scene and feel proud of Jesus for his words of comfort and liberation? And then can I experience these words as addressed to my heart?

As we've noted before in this retreat, the real fruit of the week's reflection will occur to the degree that the reflection makes its way into the background of our everyday lives. From the time we wake, until the time we sleep, we can let each and every human experience be open to being an experience of intimacy with Jesus. The readings will help us get there. The more those words of Jesus penetrate my heart, the more I will experience every part of my life addressed—my ambivalence, my fears, my hungers, my efforts to be merciful and a peacemaker.

- Do I feel joined to Jesus in this or that act of my day, drawing nourishment that bears fruit?

- Can these words expose moments when I go away sad because I can't bring myself to be heroic in this or that choice, when my possessions are at stake?

- Can I imagine being judged at the end of time by
  how I deal with the seemingly unimportant people
  in my life today?

- Do I walk through my day as though I'm in search
  of a treasure or fine pearl—where everything else
  pales in importance in comparison to the desire to
  give myself completely to being with the one I love
  in his mission?

- Can I give him thanks this very morning or
  afternoon or evening—in these events—for his
  liberation, for the blessedness he is revealing to me
  about my poor but humble spirit?

Give thanks each evening before I go to sleep for the growing
presence of Jesus' spirit in my day, drawing me to greater freedom and joy and being with him in giving my life away.

And please consider sharing any graces from this week
with others making the retreat by going to the online retreat
page and clicking on the "To Share" link. This could allow
many other people to profit from the graces offered you.

For the Journey: Listen Carefully

We are in the midst of a courtship process. Jesus is walking
through the villages of his time and into the living spaces of
our own hearts. He continues performing those acts of healing and feeding, teaching and comforting, which are meant to
impress us and encourage us to follow him.

This week we sit down with him on the side of a hill, while
he sets out his personal inauguration address. He has revealed
himself as the one who fulfills the prophet Isaiah's foretelling
of the one who would have the Spirit upon him to bring good
news and recovery. Jesus now foretells how he sees himself
living as well as those who would be so attracted to him so as
to live like him.

We sit down with the other disciples and watch their reactions to this strange new way of living and interacting. Perhaps you see some who smile at such simplicity and naïveté. Perhaps you catch sight of a few faces who begin glowing with excitement as they want to hear more of what fires their imaginations.

You may visualize Jesus turning to you when he says, "Happy are you when you are a peacemaker or person of mercy." It is not a demand but a gentle invitation to do what is good for you. While others may quietly scoff or snicker at these words of his new way, you yourself might feel a pull toward this manner of following and revealing the Master.

There might be one or two things you may wish that he had not said as you listened. You may resist or find personal difficulty in imagining yourself being meek or poor of spirit. It is very humbling and blessed to pray with our resistances to his teachings. He knows our ways, and our ways are so deeply influenced by the ways of this earth and our cultures.

The one who is doing the inviting does so with full awareness of our ways; he embraces them and calls us through them. We are of this earth and he asks us to learn a radically new way that is as strange to us as walking and living on another planet. We continue watching and listening and letting him come closer so that the transition to the new planet will not be so strange or even absurd. We learn, as did the early members of his way, to embrace our real fears and questions about following Jesus so intimately. His teachings are meant to put us all in the tensions with which the early followers found themselves. These tensions are caused by our having lived so long according to our own cultural and personal inauguration addresses.

The call of Jesus to each of us is not an impatient imperative but rather a timely invitation to a relationship that will slowly move our desires to live those ways that moved others to distance themselves from the Master. Perhaps as we pray this week, we find fewer and fewer listeners remaining on the hillside. We have felt the inclinations to silently slip away having wonderful excuses and with great promises and intentions to return.

Here we are, though, still listening to his words, listening to our own inner words. The prayer for us this week remains. Is there a call welling up in me out there?

In These or Similar Words . . .

Dear Jesus,

In prayer today I read the Gospel from John. In it you invite me to stay joined to you and you say that together we will produce fruit. The desire in me is so deep to do that. How? Where? What will we do together? I reread these too-familiar passages in the Gospel, but now they come to life in a new way. Stay joined with you and you will stay joined with me. Together we will produce fruit. It's a powerful invitation and I want to accept it.

I picture you on a hillside talking to us in the crowd. You came and brought your message to the poor—to them—but I can see the poor you are talking to and I am one of them. Now you are offering us life, a life with you. You see us, not as a crowd, but as individuals, each struggling to be freer people, poor in spirit and wanting something more—wanting to be closer to you. And you give us an answer to that desire. You offer us yourself, your friendship, and ask us to join in your life of serving the poor—others like ourselves.

Dear Jesus, you see me as a captive who needs to be set free of my limitations, my selfishness, and my seeking of the easy way out. I feel you there for me, next to me, as I begin to sense how I want to serve you and how I need to be free to do that.

I feel you accepting of me, with all of my limitations, all of my shortcomings. I am so aware of them all, and yet right there in the midst of my weaknesses, you accept me and love me and ask me to join with you. I feel the pull of your invitation and I feel my love for you growing deeper. Your care and gentle manner are so attractive—how could I turn down your invitation? Yes, I want to go with you. But somewhere inside I feel the voice asking, "What will it cost me?"

I love what you say about being merciful, helping those who grieve, and being a peacemaker. Yes, I will do that with and for you. Then you ask me to be humble, and I want to balk at that. Humble? Poor of spirit? And yet I know so well that when I am capable and self-sufficient and independent, I don't turn to you, my loving friend, for help. Now I want something different—to turn to you more, always, for help and support and friendship. Teach me to be humble. Show me what it means to be poor of spirit. I don't always know how to change the way I live to become more poor, but that is my desire now. Please show me how to be humble. Give me the grace to want to be humble. Let me bring all the ways I resist being poor and humble to you. I know only that this is the way to be closer to you and your love.

Our world teaches us one way: you offer another. I am so deeply immersed in this world and I feel myself resist, and yet the flame in my heart is growing stronger as I watch you and love you more each day. Teach me. Thank you for loving me so much that you invite me to go with you.

Scripture Readings

Luke 4:14–21
Matthew 5:1–16
Matthew 13:44–46
Luke 6:46–49
Matthew 25:31–46
John 15:1–7

"He healed our diseases
and made us well."

—Matthew 8:17

Jesus Heals

Guide: Coming to Know the Healer

As we continue to grow in our desire to know Jesus more intimately, we come to a week of reflection on Jesus the healer. This week's prayer brings us to see several important aspects of God's love for us in Jesus. Most of all, we enter more deeply into the heart of this *man for others* and come to understand a love that heals.

This is not about contemplating the divine power of Jesus or how he repaired the bodies or lives of a number of people during the three years of his public ministry on earth. This is about our coming to know more deeply this week another aspect of who Jesus is.

Jesus is able to heal because love heals. The more complete the love, the more profound is the healing. Jesus' love is penetrating. He doesn't hold back any of himself in loving. He is not put off by disfigurement or fear of contamination or even religious conventions that place limits to his loving. He is not afraid to touch and touch deeply. His heart is full of compassion. Jesus can so suffer with the one who suffers that he enters into the depths of—even the roots of—the pain of those he loves. Jesus loves so deeply he can understand and love the paralysis that causes the paralysis, the blindness that underlies the blindness, the leprosy that breaks out in leprosy. Jesus heals by embracing. Jesus embraces the inner illness that seems so untouchable or rigid or hidden in the darkness of denial. Jesus can love the whole person into *wellness*, precisely because he loves the whole person in *brokenness*. With such great love Jesus the lover can say, "Get up and start moving freely again," or "Open your eyes and see again."

This week we let ourselves become more deeply fascinated by, enthralled with, the way Jesus loves. The readings are our entry points into being present to those scenes of healing. However, the depth and power of our prayer this week, in the background moments throughout our days, will be *how we become more and more aware of how Jesus loves in the real scenes of our life*. We will come to see the meaning of love and the concrete ways we are being drawn to be with Jesus in his loving. Who throughout our day seems diseased or paralyzed or dysfunctional or blind or outcast by others? What external disorder or inner infection needs penetrating, embracing love? And, especially where I can't imagine myself loving that deeply and completely—because I taste the inner resistance of it—I can imagine Jesus' desire to love and heal.

Use the resources to begin the week and enter deeply into it. Please feel free to go to the online retreat page to offer your images and graces to others making the retreat.

Each and every day this week, we can be amazed and in awe as the Healer reveals the limitless love of his heart.

Some Practical Help for Getting Started This Week

Getting started these weeks involves listening, watching, and experiencing the feelings that come to us. We want to make the movement from reading the Gospel passages to fixing those scenes in our imagination, to letting healing become the lens through which we view the people and circumstances of our daily lives. And then the grace will be in our nightly expression of gratitude and intimacy with Jesus.

Larry Gillick, SJ, says it so well in this week's "For the Journey": "In Christ there is the freeing from and the freeing for, the healing from and the healing for." By this time in the retreat, we are experiencing the liberation that has been offered us. As we are drawn into deeper intimacy with Jesus, we are experiencing how we are set free to be one with him in loving the way he loves—completely. This is what happens with lovers. With each and every week, we are watching as Jesus shows us who he is, and we fall more deeply in love with him, and we want to be *with* him. *Attraction* always draws to *the desire for closeness.* And with each week's movements and graces, we want more and more to be *like* Jesus.

Jesus heals to set hearts free to give glory to God and then to be more responsive to God's movement in hearts that are free to say "yes" to give their self in service of others. When we are loved and healed—as all of us have been—our lives are not our own any more. We have become reoriented. We become *for others—and precisely with Jesus for others.*

We get started this week mindful of the power of these movements and their ultimate goal. This retreat is about letting God so work in us to liberate and transform how we *choose*—in fact, *how we make the most fundamental and most ordinary choices of our lives.*

Each morning, as I prepare my mind and heart for the day's reflection on Jesus as lover and healer, and each night, as I give thanks and reseal the intimacy of my growing relationship with Jesus, I can't avoid experiencing how this very process is liberating. The movements of these exercises can't help but change the way I make the smallest of choices about how I live.

As I realize what graces might be offered me as I watch and contemplate Jesus, I can ask with great focus throughout the week for the graces that are arising in my desires.

For the Journey: After the Healing

In praying this week with the pictures of Jesus curing people, we are offered opportunities to reflect on how his curing us has taken hold in the whole of our lives. It is too simplistic to see Jesus only as a physical healer. Physical well-being is not the definitive sign of God's loving care or presence.

When we consider Jesus' healing of a person in the Gospels, watch the afterness, the "What then?" of the encounter. Jesus sends the person from some inner condition to the outer world and relationships around him or her. The most basic energy of God's will as expressed in the life and words of Jesus is, "I have come that they may have life and have it to the full." Being physically healed is a sign of being freed from not really having life to the full.

What we watch and pray with this week is the process of Jesus' bringing this world to life in him and how each of us is meant to come to life for this world. The Spiritual Exercises are a gift from God given to us through the struggles of Ignatius to free himself from the inner diseases so that he might seek and do the will of God in living outwardly alive.

The will of God is not a mystical needle in a cosmic haystack for which we can spend our lives searching. That would not be a loving God who would play with us like that. His will is to love us and bring us to full life. Love, by its very nature, urges revelation. It is God's will that we trust that what we faithfully choose to do. For our part, we struggle, like Ignatius, to be honest about those areas of our lives that are not alive, which are diseased and need the healing touch of Jesus. This is why we take such long lingering views of Jesus bringing others to life and this life includes the "What next?" the follow-up, the follow-through, the following.

In Christ there is the freeing from and the freeing for, the healing from and the healing for. Jesus heals not for the personal contentment of the man or woman of faith but rather for the personal completion that is received in joining his mission of bringing others to life. The will of God is that each of us be healed from not believing in God's love for us and for this world. Our blindness, our paralysis, our being deaf, our being dead, are all embraced by Christ, and he takes away our good excuses that once confined and defined us. He is sent to touch us and then send us to embrace this bent world.

In praying this week, we pray with the many calls of those who were in such need for his healing. We pray with the many calls he offers us to go out, go beyond, and go into the world around us. Is there a call from you and to you in there?

In These or Similar Words . . .

Dear Jesus,

I feel so strongly the power of your love and of your healing. I see you from my spot in the crowd and watch how you touch and love so many, curing and healing. I am so afraid to ask for healing, to risk your love. But the kindness and warmth in your voice pulls at me and invites me to ask. I look in your kind eyes, and suddenly I am not in a crowd of people but we are alone. You are looking at me and listening with total attention as I ask: Lord, you have the power to make me well if only you want to.

If only you want to. Your love for me is so complete and so deep that healing me is a part of all of that. Your ability to heal me and your love for me are both so complete, if only I can accept that. I feel the warmth of your hand on me, healing the ways I am crippled, loving the ways I am crippled, and inviting me to love my own imperfection.

Now I feel your healing love flooding through me. I feel your strength where I have none and your courage where mine is so lacking. Your healing comes with an invitation: "Join me." May I join you? Can I stay by your side and continue to feel that love and courage? Help me to be healed from my unbelief. Help me to realize that my being crippled is sometimes a choice I make, a choice that is crippling in itself.

Please, dearest friend and brother, Jesus. Heal me from the many ways I am unable to love and accept others. Heal me from the many ways the pains of my past life create such scars on my ability to care for others. Teach me how to be with you, side by side, healing and caring for people with the love I receive from you. Most of all, teach me how the power of your love can allow me to forgive those you love so much.

I treasure your love for me and your companionship with me in this journey of healing and forgiveness. Thank you for the many ways you love me and heal me.

Scripture Readings

Luke 4:31–37
Luke 5:12–15
Luke 5:17–28
Luke 13:10–17
Luke 18:35–43

A firm resolve never to profit from,
or allow ourselves to be suborned by,
positions of power deriving from privilege,
for to do so, even passively,
is equivalent to active oppression.
To be drugged by the comforts of privilege
is to become contributors to injustice
as silent beneficiaries of the fruits of injustice.

—Pedro Arrupe, SJ,
Superior General of the Society of Jesus,
Men for Others,
Address to the Tenth International Congress
of Jesuit Alumni of Europe,
Valencia, Spain, July 31, 1973

WEEK 24

Jesus Confronts Religious Leaders

Guide: Tension and Hypocrisy

Over the past eleven weeks we have contemplated the life of Jesus. He has shown himself to us in the context of our examining his mission and our own way of life. We have considered two ways of desiring in Week 17 and three kinds of responses in Week 18. In contemplating his calling his disciples, in Week 21, we considered three degrees of being with Jesus.

We now begin to contemplate how all this is played out in Jesus' life. We begin to feel the tension developing as Jesus speaks more and more prophetically. As we read the readings, we grow in awe at his freedom and clarity. He sees through hypocrisy and names it. The fear of reprisal doesn't in any way deter him from denouncing injustice. Jesus knows what happens to prophets. His words come out of the purest of poverty and indifference. He can surrender to humiliation and rejection and death itself, for he has become a humble servant of his mission.

This week we want to enter into the tension and the freedom. We want to keep asking to be drawn to him as we let him show us this prophetic part of his spirit. He is the teacher, the healer, and the one who calls for justice, even at the cost of his own life.

In all the background moments of our week, we can be imagining the words of Jesus that would confront hypocrisy. We can feel the tension and the freedom of his spirit there. We can let it address our hearts. We can speak with Jesus about our love and admiration for him, and our desire to be placed with him in a life that does justice.

The helps to get started, "For the Journey," and prayers will be especially helpful this week. The photo can inspire us this week and become a symbol of our desire to be free for mission. The late Fr. John Cortina, SJ, one of the inspiring Jesuits in El Salvador, preaching in front of a mural with an image of Archbishop Óscar Romero, can remind us all week of how the following of Jesus continues to show forth in heroism and martyrdom, in the name of justice, even in our day.

Some Practical Help for Getting Started This Week

We are all inspired by a *hero*—someone who shows great courage in risking self in accomplishing a tremendous goal. This week we let ourselves be inspired by the heroic in Jesus. It is his spirit that has inspired and empowered the vision and freedom of countless martyrs and witnesses down through the ages and even in our day.

To get started, we need to read the readings and really experience what it took for Jesus to confront the religious leaders of his day. To enter more deeply into an example of the powerful inspiration of the prophetic spirit in our time we might rent three movies: *El Salvador* and *Romero* and *Roses in December.* They would offer some dramatic images from one country's struggle for justice to complement the Gospel scenes—especially in the lives of Archbishop Óscar Romero and Jean Donovan, who along with three American nuns, was brutally murdered in El Salvador.

We are approaching the part of Jesus' life that will call him to journey to Jerusalem and surrender his life. He does this not as a passive and meaningless victim of some insane force. Jesus spoke what he had become—God's Word, for us.

We are also moving through these weeks of the retreat with part of our minds and hearts reflecting on how we will be changed by this experience. Our desire to choose more freely—which is being shaped by our growing admiration and love for Jesus—becomes more and more concrete. This week we continue to let ourselves be drawn to Jesus, because our desire to *be with him* will indeed transform our day-to-day lives.

As we wake each day, we recall his prophetic clarity, how he came to proclaim liberty to captives and to bring good news to the poor as their advocate. During the day, in all the background times, we will be more sensitized to see the *forces at work* that are contrary to religious values, contrary to the dignity of human life, contrary to justice. As we read the paper or listen to the news, we will better hear the cry of the poor in world and local headlines, and we will be more attuned to the voices that speak for values and justice. Each evening we can speak our thanks to Jesus for showing us who he is for us and how he is, even now, drawing us to be with him in being women and men for others.

Please consider sharing the graces you receive with others making this retreat by going to the online retreat Web page and clicking on the "To Share" link. Graces given to you may help in ways you will never know, in building up the courage and faith of others.

For the Journey: Praying with the Man of God

We pray this week with a man in conflict, not within himself but with those who hear him as new and different.

The Pharisees and their scribes, as the religious leaders of their times, were being faithful to their ancient and well-lived traditions. They were well-trained in their scriptures and the art of searching them for their depth of wisdom and meaning. Jesus rises from the same religious traditions and enters the discussions with the Pharisees with a new way of interpreting those same scriptures. Jesus is seen as a rebel and a disturber of the people. It is their fidelity's meeting that personal fidelity of Jesus that causes the tensions that lead so frequently to Jesus' being confronted in the pages of the Gospels.

We could easily pray with such opposition to Jesus' teachings in our own lives. During these past weeks we have prayed with the history of our resistance to his ways. This ongoing tension between our ways and his will always form the drama of our own following of him.

This week, it is more appropriate, however, to pray with Jesus as a peaceful and self-accepting man of God. Ignatius moves us to contemplate the freedom that Jesus possesses stemming from his having heard and having believed who he is in the eyes of his heavenly Father. He knows who he is and he knows too the holiness of the ancient traditions and practices that his teachings build on, yet challenge. We are watching and listening to a person of fidelity both to himself and to his conflicts.

He is free to hear the arguments against him and his ways. He desires the engagements with his opponents as he was eager to engage the sick and needy around him. Fidelity is not being stubborn. Jesus fearlessly stays open to the dialogue and even to the threats. Rather, the word is *passionate.* For Ignatius, the word *passionate* means a fiery openness to whatever is offered. We consider this man of passion, of intense, open-hearted, open-handed availability for him to be reverenced as well as offended.

In watching and listening to Jesus this week, we ask God for that kind of self-acceptance that frees us from both the inner conflicts and the fears of being rejected by those who may fear us and our freedom. Self-acceptance is more than a psychological conclusion. We are invited to accept the created, the redeemed, and the blessed-and-sent self who has found acceptance in Christ. In this sense and in the eyes of the world, we too, then, would join Jesus in being new and different, rebellious, and a disturber to our culture as he was to his.

In These or Similar Words . . .

Dear Jesus,

How do you do it? I have prayed this week with the readings and I watch, as your encounters with the religious and political leaders grow tenser. I see how you increasingly threaten them, as you grow more critical of them. And what draws me to you even more is the calm peace you have about you.

I watch you face the people in authority who don't trust you. You look them in the eye, confront them, and raise your voice. I am usually frightened by anger but not your anger here. It seems right. You seem so clear on what is right and what is wrong, and you have no fears about your own safety. It seems as though your only thought is to be true to the person God called you to be.

Your own sense of who you are has freed you to serve God in ways I can't imagine. I feel so limited by my fears and trepidation, and yet so drawn to the freedom I see in you, the freedom to serve God.

Help me, Jesus, to see where God is calling me to serve. I see so many things that are wrong or unjust in the world, in my country and city, even in my family. But I am afraid. How can I change things? How can I learn to confront? Maybe more important, what is God calling me to do?

As I watch you, dear friend Jesus, I grow in love for your strength and the freedom you have in the way you serve God. I am so drawn to that. I want that ability to serve God unencumbered by all of my fears. You seem to have such a sense of who you are and how you are being called by God to serve. I want so much to be courageous enough to confront the structures and authorities I see that are wrong. But Jesus, I'm afraid. Confronting brings back frightening memories that need healing, and I need to feel your love and freedom to serve as the core of my own. I've never been a fighter, only someone who slinks from conflict.

But as I stay with you this week, I see that the constant confrontations with the authorities seem to give you a sense of greater peace and firmer resolve. It's as if it is becoming clearer to you exactly who you are and what God is calling you for.

That's what I want, Jesus. I want to be able to put my head up and, like you, look people in the eye as I challenge them. I want the courage to speak up for those who need help. I want the courage to stay by your side in all of this; to work like you, for justice; and to bring good news to the poor.

Thank you for sharing so much of your life with me. I feel my love and my connection with you increasing as I get to know you each day. Thank you for inviting me to be with you on this journey. Give me the courage I need to walk it as you do.

Scripture Readings

Matthew 21:12–17
Matthew 21:33–45
Matthew 23:1–39
John 11:45–57

I am sending you to harvest crops in fields
where others have done all the hard work.

—John 4:38

WEEK 25

Jesus as Water, Light, and Life Itself

Guide: Who Jesus Is for Us

This week our journey with Jesus continues to grow in depth. As our desire to be with him grows, and as our choices about the way we will live our lives become clearer, it is easier to spend time in fascination with this one we love.

Three powerful scenes from John's Gospel will fill our week. They represent a profound reflection on the meaning of Jesus for the community that first read the Fourth Gospel but also for us today.

We should read the stories carefully. We need to enter into the interaction between Jesus and the characters. We want to become engrossed in each question, each misunderstanding, each turn of phrase, each rise in the level of tension, and each transformation of the people in the scene. Then we will see how carefully this proclamation of who Jesus is can come alive for our lives today.

Throughout this week, we can become more highly attuned to the dynamics of the stories, as they are part of our journey in this retreat. This week can help us pull together what has been the grace of this retreat for us so far. The woman at the well, the man born blind, and Jesus' friend Lazarus represent us and how we have experienced Jesus in this retreat.

The grace will come when I see that I have been at the well a long time and have long been thirsty. When I can name the new thirst, the Water that now satisfies that thirst, I can overcome my remaining resistance to trust. When I see that Jesus reveals himself to me by revealing me to me, thereby showing me my need for him as Savior, I will rejoice and tell the whole world too.

The grace will come when I acknowledge that my eyes have been opened. Others may not want to believe I can see, but I know I can only keep repeating it, to myself and to them. I may experience rejection by some for claiming this new vision, but in the Light I can see clearly one who has healed me, and I give him thanks and praise.

The grace will come when I experience how my deaths will not end in death but in giving glory to God. When I experience how entombed I have been, tied and bound, no longer alive, dead for a long time, I will sense the power of the command of Jesus that I come forth.

Use the resources to let these contemplations be a part of the background of each day this week. Throughout the week, we can grow in gratitude as we acknowledge who Jesus has become for us. Our choices are being confirmed, to become one with him in living our lives, in growing harmony with his love for us.

Some Practical Help
for Getting Started This Week

We can best get started this week by reading each of the three readings very carefully. They were written with such great care. These powerful portraits of Jesus reveal to us wonderful ways to discover the same presence of Jesus in our everyday lives.

The key to this week is how we let these stories enter the background of our week. The more familiar we become with the dynamics of the three encounters with Jesus, the better we will be at finding fruit in reflecting throughout the week on the dynamics of our own lives with Jesus.

If we take each story and break it open in our reflections, we will begin to see questions that we can chew all week.

Why did the Samaritan woman come to draw water at noon, the hottest time of the day? Did she want to avoid the times the other women in town came to the well? What are the places in my life where I am embarrassed, where I avoid interaction with others? What are the noonday wells of my life? Can I imagine Jesus approaching me there?

Jesus tries to reveal his thirst to her—perhaps his thirst for intimacy with her—but she puts him off. She's not worthy. It won't work. When he offers to satisfy her thirst, she puts him off. He can't satisfy what she needs, at least with this well, and without a bucket. How do I put Jesus off, with excuses, with problems, with barriers? I don't have time; I haven't done this before; my stuff's too complicated; I don't know how to find you in this mess.

When he shows her that he knows her, she knows she's in the presence of someone special—perhaps the one she has thirsted for all her life. Do I let Jesus show me that he knows and understands me? Can I find the words to say he is the one I have thirsted for all my life?

The man born blind washed the mud from his eyes in the pool called Siloam, "The one who is sent." How is Jesus a pool to wash the mud from my eyes that I might see?

As soon as he could see, his life became very difficult. People wondered whether he was the same man before they believed that he could now see. Has the restoration of my sight so changed me that others are surprised at the transformation? So much fear seems to surround the restoration of his sight. What fears do I now have to seeing clearly who Jesus is and what choices I must make to be with him?

Martha speaks profound sorrow at the death of Lazarus, but it is tinged with a touch of blaming Jesus: "Lord, if you had been here my brother would not have died." Where do I resent the losses in my life and somehow blame God for them rather than see them as places where God's glory will be revealed? Even when Jesus tells Martha, "I am the one who raises the dead to life!" she finds it hard to believe that he means now, in the case of her dead brother. Where do I doubt that Jesus can bring life?

Jesus stands before the tomb weeping. He places no barriers to his feelings about death. Could he be staring at and facing the tomb of his own death? Can I be with him there? Can I stand before and face the tombs in my daily life?

Jesus shouts the liberating words of life, "Lazarus, come forth!" How is he shouting that to me today?

Every morning this week, as I put on my slippers or robe, I will prepare for the day. And each evening, I will take a moment to give thanks for this profound journey. It is all gift. It is all about union with Jesus. It is all for God's greater glory and the service of others.

For the Journey: Reading the Signs

One of life's great discoveries is the difference between the words *possible* and *probable*. This week we continue being attracted by Jesus' signs to the person and mission of the Sign Maker. He continues to make gestures that make him and his ways possible to some and improbable to others.

The Gospel according to John has the first twelve chapters highlighting signs of not only the power of Jesus but also of his desire to provoke responses. There is always the apparently impossible to these signs. "They have no wine." "You have no bucket." "We have only five loaves and two fish, but what are they among so many?" Jesus creates discussion and opposition by moving from the impossible to the sign. There are always the surface tensions of not having with the inner tension of believing or not believing.

We are invited this week to pray with our own resolves and responses. We are hearing his call to be signs ourselves. We wonder with the woman at the well at this man who has told us everything about ourselves. He offers us more than insight: a living water that will always sustain us. "How can this be?" We know we are being given new sight to see Jesus when others do not. Is he real to us? "Show him to me and I will worship." Now we see him, now we don't. We have been raised from a deadness but is this real life? We have been in the tomb a long time. Things can seem probable, but are they at all possible in the realness of our simple lives?

The Book of Signs in John's Gospel prepares us disciples to more freely live our sign value by trusting in the possible with him who changed the alienated into a believer, blindness into faith sight, and death into life.

We pray from our skeptical side as well. Jesus' signs confounded many and they no longer followed him. He has given us hard sayings, and we wonder whether we can stay possible with him as he moves into even greater opposition and conflict. We pray with our fears as he moves from provoker to the suspected, resented, and condemned.

This week we pray with he who changes the meaning of water, light, and life for us. We pray with our attractions and our fears; we pray with our doubts and our desires to continue to follow him. "To whom shall we go? You have the words of eternal life."

In These or Similar Words . . .

Dear Jesus,

I want to stay closer to you this week, more comfortable with the things you do and the way you challenge people. I love seeing you touch, heal, and comfort so many people. At first I watched at a distance, seeing how gentle you were with other people. Then I saw how gentle you were with me. Your comforting words give me a sense of your love for me. When you want to say more challenging words, you take my hand and look right at me with a direct, calm look as you invite me into courage. I feel you draw me into a deeper friendship with you, you who have become such a close friend.

I read the Gospel about the woman at the well. I go there, in the heat of the day, when no one else is around. I just want to get the water and get out before I run into someone from town who will reject me or mock me. Instead I run into you, sitting at the side of the well as though you have been waiting for me.

You invite me to quench my thirst with a different kind of water, and suddenly I realize how much thirst and longing is inside of me. I want to make my life different, to undo the mistakes I have made. I have shut God out of my life for so many years, and it seemed as if there were no way back. And then you invite me into your water and into eternal life.

Your brown eyes are fixed firmly on mine as you acknowledge my sins. But none of my flaws matter. You have already wiped them away with your compassion. All of the reasons I have for keeping my distance from God don't matter any more. My sins, the fact that I'm not really a good person, that I've made so many mistakes, none of this matters because you have invited me into a new life.

I have a new sense of freedom, the same freedom I see in you as you break social barriers by speaking to a lowly Samaritan like me. I feel lighter somehow, and all I want to do is shout the news loudly. "Come and see!" I want to tell everyone about you, those who have rejected me and those I am afraid of. None of my fears matter anymore because I have your good news, your living water, and the freedom I see in you.

Thank you, Jesus, my loving friend. Thank you for the wonderful love and life you invite me into. Thank you for healing me, for loving me. Like the Lazarus story, you wept for me when I was separated from you, but you never stopped loving me. Let me feel what it is like to experience your freedom as you see me stumble out of the tomb and as you untie me and let me go free.

Scripture Readings

John 4:1–42
John 9:1–41
John 11:1–45

If any of you want to be my followers, you must forget about yourself. You must take up your cross and follow me. If you want to save your life, you will destroy it. But if you give up your life for me and for the good news, you will save it. What will you gain, if you own the whole world but destroy yourself? What could you give to get back your soul?

—Mark 8:34–37

Jesus Heals
His Disciples' Blindness

Guide: "I Want to See"

We come to the point in Jesus' life where his choice becomes clear. He will go to Jerusalem. He will embrace his mission. In the first Gospel to be written, Mark paints a powerful portrait of that journey. It begins as far north as Jesus travels and proceeds south to Jerusalem. It begins with a dramatic symbolic miracle. Jesus heals the blindness of a man but not instantaneously. At first the fellow begins to see, but his vision is distorted. When Jesus touches the man's eyes a second time and heals him and then asks his disciples about their vision of who he is, we understand that this journey is about opening their eyes to see who he really is and what their mission is in following him.

Along the way, Jesus predicts what will happen to him in Jerusalem three times. Three times, they misunderstand it. And three times he tells them what it means to be his disciple. Finally, as they approach the outskirts of Jerusalem, Jesus encounters another blind man and "right away the man could see, and he went down the road with Jesus" (Mark 10:52).

With this journey, this week, our sight is clarified about who Jesus is and how we can go with him to Jerusalem.

After Jesus first tells them what is to come, Peter doesn't see rejection and death in Jerusalem as the mission of Jesus. Jesus tells him he sees like everybody else, not as God sees. Jesus says that if we want to be his disciples, we have to surrender any self-absorption and *take up our cross* with him. Any desperate attempt to avoid giving our lives away is *deadly*. But placing our lives in God's hands is *life giving*. Is our journey on a path to "gain the whole world" and destroy ourselves in the process? Or is it a journey that is free, self-giving, and alive?

After Jesus tells them the second time what they can foresee in Jerusalem, he finds that they are arguing about which of them is the greatest—a very common thing for all of us to do. Jesus tells them that greatness is about *being a servant*. It is about embracing the littlest ones around us—the marginal, the defenseless, the poor. Is this the greatness I seek? What little ones do I embrace? This far down the road, is my vision becoming clearer?

As a good teacher, Jesus tells them what to look for in Jerusalem. This time their vision is still blurred by their desire for the glory that they anticipate in Jerusalem. They are caught up in competition and jealousy. Jesus tells them that their role as servants rules out that kind of behavior. With whom do I compete? How could I be at their service? When Jesus asks, "What do you want me to do for you?" can I respond, "Master, I want to see!"? What happens inside of me when, at this point in my retreat's journey, Jesus says, "Your eyes are healed because of your faith"?

Use the resources this week, particularly the Gospel texts suggested as readings. "For the Journey" offers an in-depth reflection on the week. "In These or Similar Words . . ." offers us words that can help us find our own words to speak with our Lord this week. Consider going to the online Web page of this retreat and sharing the graces you receive.

Our desire is to follow him down the road ahead. We know it will involve carrying our cross, but we now see more clearly that we are with him, as servants of his own mission.

Some Practical Help for Getting Started This Week

This week we will use all of the means we have practiced since the beginning of the retreat. We get started by reading the texts of the readings for this week. As we begin the week, we want to get these scenes deep inside us.

We will begin each day by recalling what it is we wish to become part of the background of our day and asking for the grace we desire that day. Each morning, for a very brief time, perhaps as we put our slippers or robe on, we will remind ourselves of the focus of our day and will ask *to see Jesus more clearly, to love him more deeply, that we may become one with him more completely in the everyday choices of our lives.* We are focusing on this journey to Jerusalem, and we want it to become concrete for us each day. We are desiring to be able to see and to follow Jesus down that road. So each morning and throughout the day—as I drive to work, begin my day, walk from this place to that, reach for the phone, return home, in the dozens of in-between times of the day—I can say, simply and briefly, "Dear Jesus, I want to be with you. Show me the way today. I so want to see."

It should be easy this week to let these reflections interact with the everyday elements of our lives. It should not be difficult to discover the image of Jesus or his journey deep into the mystery of life and death itself. We can let every experience we encounter in the week, in which there might be some element of conflict, misunderstanding, resistance, dishonesty, even cruelty, show us his path. God calls Jesus to make the journey—to not hold back. God promises Jesus that he will fall into the hands of a loving God. But, along the way, he must let go of self-absorption. He must say "yes" to the poverty and powerlessness he is experiencing. He is journeying into vulnerability to rejection, even humiliation. Our eyes are opened throughout our day as we recognize *these elements there*. Wherever we encounter moments in our experience—ours or of those around us—experiences of darkness, loss, struggle, pain, violence, injustice, any kind of death at all, we clearly see how deeply Jesus journeys into our human experience.

It should be easy to be attentive to moments of blindness in my heart this week. I can be very sensitive to the times I will feel *resistance* rise up in my heart or stomach. It says, "I don't want to do this." It says, "No." It says, "How do I avoid this?" I can look for the experiences of *competition* I encounter. I can be more highly aware of the dynamics that define what greatness is. I can look at and name the instances of *struggle to be servant for others* in my day.

All of this doesn't take more time. *It takes more attention.* Each evening, as I get ready to go to bed, I can recall the movements and reflections and insights of the day, and I can give thanks. This is so important. With growing familiarity and growing tenderness, I *seal the day* with words that express what I saw and understood about the mission of Jesus and the invitation he makes to me to be with him in this journey of self-donating love.

Images and *gestures* are important to support our prayer. Is there a cross or crucifix anywhere in my home? If not, this may be the time to buy one and put it up. If there is one in my home, I can be conscious of looking at it this week and letting it be a symbolic *link* and *support* for the reflections that begin and end my day. This could be a time to use a simple gesture to express, with my body, what I'm trying to say with my words. For one brief *minute* I can open my hands, palms up, and simply hold them there, and let them express all that is in my heart that says surrender, trust, acceptance, desire for intimacy with and togetherness in his mission, the choices forming within me, my growing "yes." All of us have time for that one minute each day, perhaps several times in the day. It will make a powerful difference in sealing the gifts we are receiving this week of clear vision.

For the Journey: The Shock of New Vision

There have been some recent studies and articles concerning the difficulties that blind people have when recovering their sight. Living for a long time without being able to visually see allows blind people to adapt in such a way that seeing again is not always the blessing it would seem to be. Recovery of sight means new adapting, and that newness can be frightening and paralyzing.

We are praying this week with Jesus giving physical sight to two different people and a different kind of sight to his disciples. This new sight for them is traumatic as any recovery of physical sight might be.

Jesus is moving slowly to Jerusalem, his destiny, and he reminds his followers that his identity and destiny are wrapped up together with their own. They resist, of course; they have other plans, of course. They are being asked to receive the vision of who they are and what they are called to be and do. We watch them having problems adjusting to this new sense and sight.

We have been receiving, or recovering, sight these past weeks of watching and listening to the Christ of God. The more intimately we allow him to be with us, the more tensions can arise. Attraction and resistance struggle within us, as with his earliest followers. There are implications to his getting into our hearts and lives, as there were with those whom he first called. He makes it very clear that if we really see him, then we will also see ourselves. This awareness can lead to self-cancellation or self-acceptance in him. We have prayed with these familiar tensions these past weeks. Now Jesus ups the ante.

238 Jesus Heals His Disciples' Blindness

What are we to do with this accepted self? As they moved closer to the place of his final destiny and dignity, the disciples were more inclined to take the Jerusalem bypass and not go into the city-traffic of treachery and betrayal. Jesus has totally accepted himself as the Christ and he hears the call to lay down his life as a gift from his Father. He has made it clear to his followers that their self-donation is the ultimate way of following and extending him and his mission.

So recovery of sight for the disciples and for ourselves, while it is a blessing, takes some deeper recovery-time. Following Jesus into our own Jerusalems of fidelity causes us to question. All our questions of "What?" and "How?" echo the worries of his first questioning friends. The closer we allow him to come, the more we might wonder where the bypass is for us. We pray this week with him and his frail flock. We are there with them and with our truth. Do we want clear sight, recovery of vision, to stay faithful in following him? We pray for the freedom from and the freedom for, and there is much of both for which to pray this week.

Is there still a call out there and in there?

In These or Similar Words . . .

Dear Jesus,

How blind can they be? I read the stories of the apostles listening to you talk about what it means to enter your kingdom. Entering it means a trial, beating, humiliation, and death. But the apostles quit listening after they heard the word *kingdom*, and the only response they have is to ask whether you will save them special places in this kingdom. I get annoyed at how dense they are and how insensitive.

Where is their support of you? You've just told them how you are going to die, and they ask whether they can get a good spot in the kingdom. But you give the same message over and over: Be a slave, not a master. Be the servant of others. What will you gain if you own the world but destroy yourself? What could give you back your soul? If you want a place of honor, you must become a slave and serve others.

Oh, wait. You weren't just talking to your apostles? I see once again that these words are also for me. I think I forgot to listen. I think I forgot to support you, my friend, as you turn to me for my love. I feel the increasing tension as you move closer to Jerusalem. I want to be there for you, but I'm not good around conflict, Jesus. I want to blend into the crowd and support you from afar.

Let me listen again. You are asking me to let go of the idea that I can somehow master complete control over my life. You invite me to trust you more and let you help me with my struggles. Every time I am willing to admit that I don't have to do it alone, I move closer to embracing the limitations that bring me closer to you. Every time I accept the humility of my own imperfections, am I not gaining myself instead of the world that rejects you?

I am at a crossroads in my life, dear friend, Jesus. I can't continue my life the way it has been, and that frightens me. I know I want to change, but I struggle with this alone until I remember that you will be with me in this. It means giving up control and trusting you. It means accepting that you are my Lord and giving up the god of perfection and success I have followed for so long.

I come before you with my hands open, asking for help. In the quiet, I feel you with me even if my words are simple ones. Be with me, Lord. I have been so deaf to your message. Heal me. I have been so blind to all the things you have wanted to share with me. Heal me. Thank you for coming into my life in this powerful way.

Scripture Readings

Mark 8:22–37
Mark 9:30–37
Mark 10:32–52

Do you understand what I have done?
You call me your teacher and Lord,
and you should, because that is who I am.
And if your Lord and teacher has washed your feet,
you should do the same for each other.
I have set the example,
and you should do for each other
exactly what I have done for you.

—John 13:12–15

Jesus Gives Us His Body and Blood

Guide: His Example, Broken and Given

This week we come to see and experience the ritual culmination of what Jesus' life has been about and what it will forever mean. For the one accused of "eating and drinking with sinners," this is his last supper on earth. This meal represents a way for us to remember and celebrate who he is for us. It is a covenant in his love that both nourishes us for our mission and gives us the example of servant love that marks our identity.

This week we go there to that scene to watch and listen. We become a part of the experience as a person in the scene. Like participants in the annual Passover memorial of the liberation from slavery in Egypt, we enter this scene as though it were happening to us.

Jesus takes his life in his hands and gives it to us. So that we will never forget the meaning of his life for us, the bread of this meal is his body—taken, blessed, broken, and given. The wine is his blood—poured out for the forgiveness of our sins. When he says, "Do this and remember me," we know he wants us to never forget, but we also know he is calling us to

241

be taken, blessed, broken, and given, that our lives might be poured out in service of others.

When he takes off his outer garment and wraps a towel around his waist, we can sense Jesus knows the time has come for him to fulfill his mission. As we let him wash our feet, the whole of our retreat, up to now, is summed up in this sign of his love for us. Our prayer to be with him in his mission is now granted as he lovingly gives us our mission in this example of his servant love. With him, we have become *transformed*—for others in the same way he is for us.

Throughout this week, from morning to night, in all the background times, the mystery of what it means to be broken and given, to be poured out in service to others, comes alive in our thinking, our desiring, and our gestures.

Use the resources this week for prayer and reflection. We pray to simply *be with Jesus*—so we might not miss the full power of his gift to us, so we can let it penetrate our hearts all week.

Some Practical Help for Getting Started This Week

We have come to a place in our journey where we can feel the effects of our praying, week after week, to see Jesus more clearly, to love him more dearly, that we might follow him more nearly, in our everyday lives. Our desire to be placed with Jesus, and the gifts of clarity about and freedom for his mission, come together in this contemplation of the Last Supper. He has shown us his life from the very beginning and invited us in, to understand and be attracted to his surrender to God, more and more. We are ready to be with him in the final days of his life. Our desire and prayer now is simply *to be with him, in compassion and love*, as he gives his life away for us.

We begin by reading the familiar accounts of the Last Supper. In the washing-of-feet scene, John paints a picture of the whole meaning of the Eucharist, the whole meaning of our discipleship, in one gesture that reveals the meaning of Jesus' gift of himself to us, as servant.

It is important that we let these powerful images become a part of the background of our lives this week. We will move through our week with the image of Jesus breaking bread with and passing a cup of wine around to his disciples. Perhaps with the photo of the Holy Thursday foot washing in our imagination all week, we will be very conscious of this image of Jesus as foot washer.

Throughout the week we can feel and express our gratitude. We can experience, in the midst of very hectic and messy times, a peace the world cannot give. All week—whether we are driving or walking from one place to another, or pouring a cup of coffee, or simply pausing to catch our breath—we can hear him say, "I have given you an example; do this in memory of me." He is broken and poured out, to completely give himself to our very human struggle that we might be whole and ourselves become bread for our world. He washes our dirty feet to show us we need not hold any part of ourselves away from his loving touch, that we might not fear to touch others with his own gentle, compassionate embrace.

The more we let the concrete events and movements of our week connect with these mysteries, the more powerful this contemplation will become. Each meal, each act of generosity or service, each gesture of acceptance of another, each "yes" this week, can place us intimately back into these scenes for a moment of *union*.

Perhaps the reflection will be sealed with a special meal we plan with our family or loved ones. Perhaps we can plan to change our routine for an hour this week and reach out to touch, hold, comfort someone who needs it this week. Perhaps this week we will pause and put in writing our own "In These or Similar Words . . ." to express our gratitude.

Please consider sharing some experience, some grace this week, with others making the retreat. You can do this by going to the online Web page of the retreat and clicking on the *A Place to Share* link. The gifts we receive are given for the building up of the whole body of Christ.

Each morning and each night this week, we can begin and end each day with the assurance that the one who began this journey in us will bring it to fulfillment in the graces he desires to give us, for God's glory and the service of others.

For the Journey: "Do This in Memory of Me"

This week we are watching Jesus fulfill his Father's loving plan for him and ourselves. We are invited to listen in to an intimate discussion as he leaves the Last Supper he has with his close friends. In Luke 22:24, a slight argument arises about which of them will be the greatest. So human of them—and his response spins them around and ourselves as well.

The greatest ones usually sit at table and the lesser serve, "But I am among you as One Who serves." He has said it; said that which he had lived all their days together.

We then turn to the thirteenth chapter of John's Gospel and we see the Servant of God and humankind with a towel wrapped around him and kneeling before these friends, washing their feet. We pause with Jesus at the feet of Peter, who resists this humiliation. We watch the eyes of Jesus looking at his dear friend. Peter has followed Jesus from the humbling experiencing of Jesus telling him where and how to catch fish and has been confounded many times since. This might be too much though. Jesus invites him again to keep coming after him. "Let me wash your feet."

The Servant is beginning his finest revelation in these final scenes of the great play of salvation. He has given them a simple way to remember him and his undying love in sharing with them the Bread of Life. He has also given them a way to live that remembrance by inviting them to wash one another's feet in whatever manner that may be and to "do this in memory of me." The Servant is asking all his friends to follow him these days as he completes his ministry of loving all of humankind.

For us, these days are for very serious watching and listening. Ignatius invites us to come close and let our imaginations bring us prayerfully into Jesus' presence. We can be on our knees next to Peter or sitting at table breaking bread and remembering the great deeds of the Passover. We let him wash our feet, or maybe we, too, resist that gentle gesture of tenderness. Perhaps we join in the discussion about our own desires for greatness and not for being a servant at the table of his sisters and brothers.

In These or Similar Words . . .

Dear Jesus,

"Lord, you can't mean me!" That's my reaction when I read the story of that last Passover meal with your friends. I am one of your friends, and as I sit around that table, so full of love and admiration for you, I feel disconcerted when you talk about one of us betraying you. "You can't mean me!" I want to call out along with Judas. How could I ever betray the one who loves me so endlessly?

I am so moved by your humanness at this meal. The story begins by saying how you had always loved your followers and you loved them until the end, and I feel it tonight, in such an intimate setting with you. You had loved us all, those who had followed you so closely from the beginning and those of us who hung back, waiting until we could be sure you were really going to save us.

Now all of us are gathered around your table, and you say that we, your closest friends, will betray you. How sad you look when you say that. How distracted you look as you think about the days ahead. I want to be with you in your apprehension and anxiety. I want to stay with you and support you, dear friend, because I sense your fears. Most of all, I want to reassure you that I won't betray you.

Then you take off your cloak and begin to wash our feet. Please, Lord, not my feet! They are so smelly and dirty and my nails are ragged. I like to keep them hidden in my sandals, not exposed to anyone, especially you. But you are so gentle as you take my feet from where I have tucked them under my garment and wash them clean. The moment you bend deeply over my newly washed feet and kiss them, I realize that the places where I can let you love me the most deeply are the places where I am embarrassed, the parts I want to hide from others, my weaknesses.

You ask if we understand what you did. You have served us by washing our feet. Your kingdom is about service, not about being pampered. Do this for one another, you say. Finally, I think I am beginning to understand what you have been talking about for so long. It's about taking care of one another, washing one another's feet, and serving one another in the most humble of ways. You have anointed my feet with your kiss and sent me on this journey to follow in your footsteps.

Can I follow you? I'm not sure, Jesus. I know that I love you and want to be like you. I am afraid that I will betray you. And I know that as sad as this makes you, my failings are the places where I need you the most. That's where you will always be with me.

But tonight, let me be with *you*, dear friend. Let me sing a hymn with you as we end this most intimate dinner and walk out into the garden to pray. Let me hold your hand through this long night ahead. I feel your love for me so deeply and I feel your invitation to join you in this journey of serving others as you have.

Thank you for inviting me. I will stay awake with you, Lord.

Scripture Readings

Matthew 26:17–30
1 Corinthians 11:23–26
John 13:1–30
Psalm 116

He suffered and endured great pain for us, . . .
He was wounded and crushed because of our sins;
by taking our punishment, he made us completely well.
He was painfully abused, but he did not complain.
He was silent like a lamb being led to the butcher,
as quiet as a sheep having its wool cut off.
He was condemned to death without a fair trial.
Who could have imagined what would happen to him?
Although he is innocent,
he will take the punishment for the sins of others,
so that many of them will no longer be guilty.
The LORD will reward him
with honor and power for sacrificing his life.
Others thought he was a sinner,
but he suffered for our sins and asked God to forgive us.

—Isaiah 53:4–5, 7–8, 11–12

Jesus Surrenders
to His Passion

Guide: Agony and Love

The photo this week was taken in the Jesuit chapel at the University of Central America in San Salvador, El Salvador. This is the Jesuit community whose members, along with their housekeeper and her daughter, were brutally assassinated. This photo is one of the stations of the cross in the chapel showing, in powerful drawings, the images of the unjust torture of innocents.

Throughout the centuries, the account of the passion of Jesus has been told to help believers understand the mystery of suffering and how Jesus' surrender defeats the power of sin and death.

At this point in our retreat, we are prepared to contemplate, in detail, the passion of Jesus. Our desire is to enter into the Gospel story and to be there with Jesus. We want to be touched by the power of this drama. The one we love and want so much to be with invites us into his story to experience his suffering, with him. The depth of our compassion for him leads to an even deeper intimacy.

Take each part of the story and experience its meaning. The garden struggle to surrender; the betrayal, the arrest, and abandonment by his disciples; the trials; the mockery, the crowning with thorns, the beating, and the way of the cross are scenes we want to become very much a part of our consciousness this week.

Throughout each day this week, we want to know the profound love of Jesus for us. As we go through the ordinary struggles of living, and face the most difficult challenges of our lives, we want to experience Jesus' solidarity with us. As we contemplate the meaning of his passion, we want to see his solidarity with all who have, are, and ever will suffer.

Use the resources this week to get started in prayer and to enter these reflections more deeply. You might consider praying the Stations of the Cross, a powerful centuries-old devotion, as a resource for our journey this week and next week. You will find an online version of the stations of the cross at the Creighton Online ministries Web site. Go to the online retreat home page and click on the "Stations of the Cross" link on the left.

Every night, let us give thanks for the graces we receive by walking through our lives more conscious of the passionate love of Jesus for us.

Some Practical Help for Getting Started This Week

We begin this week by reading Matthew's account of Jesus' passion (Matthew 26:14–27:66). It is perhaps the most familiar story in our imagination, but we can refresh it by letting it become the conscious focus of our week. This will give us vivid images that we can reflect on in the context of our everyday life this week.

The Last Supper (Matthew 26:14–30)
We reflected on the Last Supper last week. Now we focus on it as the beginning of the Passion. When we read about Judas's betrayal and Peter's promise never to deny him, we have fruit for our week. We can say, with Peter, "Even if I have to die with you, I will never say I don't know you." Throughout the week, I can become more highly conscious of times I hide how much I know Jesus.

The Garden (Matthew 26:36–56)
The garden is a powerful image of Jesus, asking his disciples to pray with him. Instead, they fall asleep. All week, in small in-between times, we can remind ourselves how much Jesus wants us to be *with him* in prayer about his Passion this week. It is important for us to see Jesus *agonize* in prayer over his surrender. His words can come to us throughout the week, to shape the way we make our choices to open ourselves to God's desires in us. To pause here to be with Jesus, as he is kissed by a betraying friend and as all his friends just run away, is a powerful communion with the one we love in a moment of deep abandonment.

The Religious Trial (Matthew 26:57–68)
Caiaphas and the religious leaders can't find an opening in their hearts for Jesus. How painful it must be for Jesus to face his failure to win over the very people he came to save. To mock his self-revelation as the indictment for his execution must have stung bitterly. All week I can focus on this part of his Passion as I observe how little he is accepted in so much of our culture today.

Judas and Peter (Matthew 26:69–27:10)
They both betray him. Judas can't perceive how God could forgive him, and he kills himself. How much Jesus must have grieved Judas's despair. Peter becomes transformed by his denial. He is able to be used by Jesus to lead in great humility and gratitude.

The Roman Trial (Matthew 27:11–21)

The Roman trial is full of ironies. He will not have his death sentence commuted. Pilate will wash his hands of the whole affair, and he will say he finds him innocent but then have him whipped and executed. We can place this trial in our memory this week as we are filled with a sense of sadness, outrage, gratitude for what Jesus went through, for me.

The Way to Crucifixion (Matthew 27:22–66)

We have provided an online prayer experience, "The Stations of the Cross," to help with this part of the contemplation on the Passion. Perhaps we can do one or two stations a day, to enter more deeply into the journey of Jesus into intimacy with our suffering. The grace we desire is to experience a growing compassion with Jesus and to know most intimately that this is all an experience of his love, *for me.*

Pray with Psalm 22. The Gospel writers must have found it to be a powerful source of inspiration about how Jesus must have used this prayer in his struggle and trust in God.

Begin each day by focusing on a part of this mystery, perhaps just for a few moments while doing something very routine (putting on slippers, while showering, while dressing). Throughout the day, recall these reflections in the background of our consciousness. Notice the mystery of the Passion of Jesus revealed in the smallest of things I see and experience in my day. End each day expressing some gratitude for what I am learning and feeling in Jesus' Passion this week.

For the Journey: Handing Over

We move with Jesus this week from the upper room where he washed the feet of his friends to the garden of obedience where he washes the earth with his bloodlike sweat. He is separated from all his support except that of his Father, with whom he now speaks face-to-face.

This week of watching moves us into a silence and a humility that all this is for me and us. The stage is cleared of all other characters and we join the apostles off to the side. They have seen him pray alone before and so drift off to wait for the next exciting installment of his and their lives. We in our turn are accustomed to this scene and we know what is coming soon. For just some time, we watch this holy man in spiritual combat. There is the inner conflict in him between his human desires to live into many exciting installments and his divinity, which has been molded to conform to his Father's will through the installments of his entire life.

There was the garden of disobedience, where this drama began. God's love for us was interrupted by our indulgent love for our selves. There was a tree from which we were not to eat. Now we watch Jesus, the new Adam, kneeling in a garden, fully aware of the good and evil around him, preparing to eat of the fruit of the tree that will bring us all back to life. Evil is about to have its way in one last grand hurrah. It is silent now and he senses a presence of the Divine Good, which he has felt before, saying that he is the Beloved. He is the Good, who will soon struggle with the forces of disobedience.

The noise of these forces intrudes on our silent watchings. Abandonment and denial become central characters, but keep your eyes on his. He receives the challenges to his goodness from the soldiers and his friend Judas. We hear him respond, "I am He." He begins his final hours of fidelity to who he knows himself to be, the Anointed, the Lamb now being led to the sacrifice.

These prayer times for us are quiet and sensitive. We make ourselves available to be impressed by the God-made-man struggling to reveal to us his faithful love and the importance of our fidelity to who we are. We also are the anointed led into our own struggles against the forces of evil. Watch his eyes as he looks for Peter during and after Peter's own encounter with his failures. Jesus is not a puppet playing out some charade of life. Listen to the noise around his silence and watch his physical responses to the abuse and violence.

With Ignatius, we have watched the Creator hand over all creation to us. In our prayer we have seen God handing over to us personal gifts and mercies of all kinds. This week we watch Jesus handing over his body and all for us. He also hands on to us the invitations to stay faithful in our own struggles between our good and our evil. Watch his eyes as they meet your own.

In These or Similar Words . . .

Dear Jesus,

I came to prayer this week to be with you in your suffering, but the first thing I saw was the photo for the week. I enlarged it and stared at it. What does this have to do with you? I want to pray about and for you, not some people I don't even know. But wait. Maybe my agenda isn't the same as yours.

I look at the photo of the drawing from El Salvador that has been made into one of the stations of the cross. I see the whip marks across the backs of this man and woman. The horrible way their bleeding hands are tied up behind them. I can see only their backs, but I realize that the woman has no top on. She must feel so vulnerable, exposed, and helpless, as her persecutors attempt to take away every shred of dignity she has.

And I stay with you in the Gospel, as you are whipped, beaten, mocked, and stripped. I watch as you struggle to surrender yourself to God. I see the fear and vulnerability you must feel, even as you give your total trust to God. You never stop praying as they batter you with questions, treat you with derision and condescension. You are with your Father in spirit, because that is the only way you know to continue this journey God sent you on.

This week I will walk with you and spend time with you in these events. I will again join you at the Last Supper and in the garden. I can't bear to watch as you are in the trial and I feel so helpless watching you, my dear friend, be pushed into this inevitable death. I know these next hours will be so terrible and I want to be there for you, but I find myself hiding with Peter, pretending I don't know you, afraid for myself.

It is only as I do the stations of the cross that I can take each step with you in this. I can walk with you each little way as I see how you have done all of this for me. How can I thank you for all you have done? I will carry those images with me throughout this week.

Then I look again at the photo of those two people. I want to be with you in your familiar story this week. But I keep thinking of the people in this photo. What happened to them? How have they been tortured and abused in your name? Your story is old and familiar to me. Theirs is not. And yet they are very real too. Where are those very real people today, Jesus? Are they still alive? Where are you, Jesus?

I look at the photo again and now I see you. How could I have missed you before? You've been there all along, standing with them as they are whipped, tied, naked, and vulnerable. You are next to them in their pain and suffering, sharing it with them, there for them, bringing them closer to God.

Thank you, Jesus, for being with them in a way I cannot. Thank you for being with me. Please, let me be with you in each moment of your agony this week, as I try to recognize you in the daily sufferings of my life.

Scripture Readings

Isaiah 50:1–7
Psalm 22
Philippians 2:6–11
Matthew 26:14–27:66

Around noon the sky turned dark
and stayed that way until the middle of the afternoon.
The sun stopped shining,
and the curtain in the temple split down the middle.
Jesus shouted, "Father, I put myself in your hands!"
Then he died.

—Luke 23:44–46

Jesus Dies for Us

Guide: Present at Calvary

We pause this week to be with Jesus in death. There are few moments of intimacy greater than the privilege of being with someone we love in the last hours of his or her life. We want to enter into the whole scene that surrounds his death and the treasured memories of the early Christian communities.

We also want to connect the meaning of Jesus' death for us with the realities of our everyday lives. We want to consciously move through our days with a heightened sense of awareness about how his death gives hope to us in our fidelity, our struggles, each day.

We begin by prayerfully reading the accounts of the scene at Calvary, in Luke and John. We enter these scenes with our own imagination—where we choose to stand, where we look, what others are saying, what we feel. It is very important to imagine the scene of taking him down from the cross and, perhaps to join in the tender cleaning of his body and the sorrowful carrying it to the tomb. The reality of death is complete.

We then can let these images fill the background of each day. From the earliest conscious thoughts of our morning to

the final concluding thoughts of our day, we want to let ourselves be touched by the death of Jesus for us.

We can be especially conscious about four areas of our
lives, to which Jesus' dying brings life and freedom:

- *Our Sin.* What we have done, what we are doing,
  and what we are tempted to do to separate ourselves
  from God, as well as all the ways we fall short of self-
  sacrificing love.

- *Our Diminishment.* Any of the ways we experience
  death: our growing older, our failing health, a
  physical or personal handicap, perhaps our own
  approaching death, experiences we have that are
  humiliating, our inadequacies, being rejected,
  financial difficulties, family stresses, a broken
  relationship, feelings of hopelessness, being
  disillusioned, the experience of depression, the loss
  of a loved one,

- *Difficulties with Others.* All the conflicts in our day-
  to-day life with difficult people that lead to mutual
  suffering, hurts, and the breakdown of unity.

- *Sin in the World.* The stories that fill the headlines
  and the day-to-day world around us: war, genocide,
  dehumanizing social structures, the unjust distribu-
  tion of the world's wealth and resources, political
  oppression, abortion, child abuse, the drug economy,
  all senseless violence, capitol punishment, bigotry,
  demagoguery, the destruction of our environment,
  dishonesty, infidelity, greed, consumerism.

Use the resources here to help with this wonderful week of
being with Jesus in his death for us. Use the stations of the
cross to enter the experience more personally.

Let us all give thanks each evening for the one who shows
us the deepest meaning of the Good News—we are free from

the power of sin and death over us. By entering our life and death completely, Jesus fell into the hands of a loving God, who raised him and us to life, redeeming all sin and death forever.

Some Practical Help for Getting Started This Week

Spending a week with Jesus at Calvary is really not very difficult. It is only a matter of focus. It is made easier by our having grown in love with Jesus over the past four months. We know we are loved sinners. We have experienced his call to join him in his mission. We have prayed with growing desire to understand his life and have felt the power of his showing us who he is, in great detail. Now we come to experience how completely human he was.

We want to be touched by the meaning of his death for us. This is not a week of theological reflection. This is a time to focus on the reality of death. Our culture rarely faces the reality of death. We distance ourselves from its experience. For all of the death and violence around us, few of us have witnessed anyone's death or touched a dead body to experience the coldness of death's lifelessness. People rarely die at home, and funeral homes take the body of a loved one fairly quickly and embalm it, put makeup on its face and hands, dress it up, and lay it out, like the person is only sleeping.

This makes it more difficult for us to imagine looking up at Jesus hanging in this terribly cruel and unbelievably painful form of execution. It makes it doubly difficult to imagine his lifeless body—the sign of the reality of his death. But as we focus each morning on our desire to be with him in his death, the graces we have received up to now will help us desire to follow him all the way to the end of his life.

As we focus on each area of our lives touched by the death of Jesus, as outlined in the guide, we can end each day with some words of gratitude. Perhaps I will want to express my feelings out loud or in writing. Each night, the expression of gratitude and intimacy grows. Perhaps I have a cross in my home, or even in my bedroom, which I can make a point of looking at or touching reverently. I might be moved to begin and end each day by tracing a cross on my forehead or over my heart as I wake up and before I sleep. This can help us consciously focus at the beginning and end of each day. With such a focus each morning and evening this week, leading to our walking through each day with a heightened awareness of the power Jesus' dying has for my faith, hope, and love today, I will never be able to look at a cross again without being powerfully reminded of the love that that sign means for me.

Use the other resources offered this week, perhaps especially "The Stations of the Cross" Web page. Let "For the Journey" and the "In These or Similar Words . . ." deepen the experience further.

The God who has brought us this far will be with us to give us more than we can ask or imagine.

For the Journey: At the Foot of the Cross

We adore you, O Christ, and we bless you, because you have embraced us while embracing the cross. When pain can make a person self-preoccupied, there walks Jesus still ministering with his gentle words and gestures. We watch him and listen to his words from the throne of the cross. "Forgive them . . ." With our imaginations we are privileged to witness God's final statement about who we are.

We have watched the violence of scourging, crowning with thorns, stumbling under the weight of the cross, and the mockery of his tormenters. Now we stand with Mary where it is not violent but safe. At the foot of the cross we can say anything we want or anything we usually say about ourselves, but those words and images pale in meaning and importance when we stand at his feet and receive what he is saying over us. We are safe here; we stand in the shadow of the cross. This shadow cancels our personal shadows, our guilt and shame. There can be some shame in our spirits flowing from our realization that it has taken all this to impress on us how loved we really have been all during our wanderings and strayings.

As he is dying, the crowds give up their jeering and move away to continue their celebrating of the Passover within the city of Jerusalem. We stay in the quiet celebration of the "new and everlasting covenant." Doubts and fears have chased most of his friends away, but he has remained faithful, and we pray to receive encouragement to our staying faithful to him. Away from the shadow of the cross, our shadows lengthen and our past infidelities incline us to not believe and not receive all that he has said about us while on his journey to the cross of cancellation. We gratefully return to our watching place, his watching place. We listen to his final benediction and pledge of faith in his Father's care.

Ignatius asks those making the Exercises to quietly receive at this second eucharistic celebration all that is offered. We look up at this cruciform altar and ponder the words of the prophet Isaiah: "Here is the Servant of the Lord. He was despised and rejected by men, a man of sorrows, and acquainted with grief and we esteemed him not" (Isaiah 53:3). We pray with our hands open to accept this mystery of our being loved this much and for always. At the foot of the cross our arguments falter and our questions about worthiness are rendered absurd. We watch, we listen, we are safe, and we find ourselves created anew, again.

"Who has believed what we have heard?" (Isaiah 53:1). We do, as we refuse to turn away with clenched hands of unworthiness and shame. We stand there until we feel safe to let them take him down. It is a holy stand we take these days of receptivity. "He was wounded for our sins, he was bruised for our iniquity; upon him was the punishment that made us whole, and by his stripes we are healed"(Isaiah 53:4).

In These or Similar Words . . .

What happened? Dearest Jesus, how did it all come to this? How is it that I am looking up at you hanging there in such incredible agony? We are huddled here in fear and disbelief. Your mother, the other women. John. A few others.

I look at you writhing in pain, unable to breathe, pulling yourself up by your nailed wrists just to gasp for air. I see you look down at me with your warm, familiar eyes veiled in pain, but it is still you. I see my dear friend, the one who has been with me through so many terrible moments in my life. Now I stand here with you, unable to do anything.

Oh, Jesus, why? Why did this happen? I know intellectually that it was to enter so fully into my life and my pain, and the pain of everyone else. But so much pain? How can one person bear it all?

I realize that as I stand here, I have been holding on to your mother's arm. Mary, who is so grieved that she is having a hard time standing. Mary, who has sat with me for so many hours as I've talked with you about my life. Now I see her almost doubled over in grief. Oh, Jesus, I don't want you to even see her pain because it will only add to yours.

She understands so well that your life is slipping away. We watch and pray and hold on to each other, this small knot of silent people who love you so much. Then I realize that as much as you mean to me, as much as I don't want you to die, I can't stand to watch you suffer either. Please God, let him be at peace. Let him pass out or die. Don't let him suffer so much.

But still, you continue to gasp and pull yourself up to breathe, in spite of the torturous pain as the nails rip down into the nerves in your arms. We listen as you pray, continue to ask the father for help, and then, finally, surrender to him. Your pale body, covered with dirt and blood trembles a final time and then is still.

Mary turns to her sister and falls into her arms, but she has no tears left. The rest of us hold one another in silence and numbness. The soldiers come and take down the body, and as it drops to the ground, Mary lifts you into her arms.

Oh, the pain in her face as she sees you! I want to help her. I want to be there for her because I know you would want me to be there. She holds your lifeless body gently and with such love, just as she did for so many years. She looks at me silently, tragically. I find a jar of water and I use my cloak to get it wet. If only I can wash the blood off your face. If only I can stop the blood from running down from the thorns. I want to do this so Mary won't have to keep seeing you in such pain. Mary Magdalene and I remove the thorns from your head and wipe your face as your mother kisses it.

Dear God, help us! Be with us in this pain and confusion. Jesus, help us to make some sense out of your suffering. Help me to see how you are a part of my suffering each day and how this act joined you to the deepest sufferings of all of us.

Thank you, God, for the gift of Jesus. Thank you, Jesus, for your life in mine. I feel it somehow, even in the midst of this.

Scripture Readings
Luke 23:26–56
John 19:16–42
Psalm 31

"Jesus isn't here!
He has been raised from death."

—Luke 24:6

Jesus Is Risen

Guide: Joy

We knew from the beginning that God's victory over sin and death was complete. Now we come to know it through the experience of new life given to Jesus. For months now we have been given the grace to become intimate friends with Jesus, who has shown us his life and who he is for us. Now we simply pray to experience *joy with Jesus* in the gift of risen life he enjoys.

Jesus really died and his dead body was laid to rest in a tomb. *The tomb is empty!* It is forever a symbol of God's power to liberate—to set us free from the power of sin and death.

Jesus is alive! And he is forever alive, with a life beyond our imagining. For the next several weeks, we want to enter into a taste of that new life. For in celebrating his liberation with Jesus, we grow in anticipation of the way that has been opened for this new life for us.

This week we contemplate, using the Scriptures and our imagination, the experience *for Jesus* of being raised from the dead and his sharing of that experience with those he loved. What inexpressible joy Jesus must have had at experiencing eternal life, as a human being! Having just experienced the depths of our suffering and death, he now knows what it will be for us to experience the life of the Resurrection.

And how he must have delighted in sharing that joy with those who suffered with him at the foot of the cross! We can only imagine what joy filled the heart of Mary, his mother, when she saw him alive. Who could have experienced *joy with Jesus* more completely?

Finally, I contemplate our risen Lord sharing his joy with me. Alive forever, and able to be with me at every moment, he still has holes in his hands and a gaping wound in his side. He still is the person whose life we have contemplated for months. The past and the present come together for us in this encounter with Jesus, risen.

All week, we will try to let ourselves walk around in the sense of Jesus, alive and with us. The more I let Jesus be alive and present in every event of my daily life, the more completely his resurrection confronts the fear, doubt, lack of courage, lack of hope, I might experience.

Use the resources here to get started and enter the movements of the week more deeply. Our awareness of Jesus' standing with us in the most mundane and ordinary moments of our days will breathe the life of his Spirit into our hearts. And we will indeed share his joy.

Some Practical Help for Getting Started This Week

We use the same practical way of proceeding in this week as we have throughout the retreat.

The Mystery We Contemplate

Here it is *Jesus alive*, enjoying God's victory over all that threatens to hold me captive.

The Grace We Ask For

Here it is to seek *joy with Jesus*. There is perhaps the least amount of self in this week. We want our joy with the one we love to be complete. It is the most profound way to enter into how his risen life transforms my life.

Our Daily Life Contemplation

This week we want to imagine those encounters between Jesus and his closest disciples and friends. Those who grieved with him at the cross are given the first gift of faith in God's power over death. I begin by imagining his showing himself alive to Mary his mother. I move during the week to his showing himself fully alive to me personally.

The Daily Means

Each morning, among the first things I do, is pause to focus on the grace I desire this week. As I move through the various commitments of my day, I let myself stay conscious of a lighter spirit within me, more deeply aware that nothing can separate me from the love of God. I try, at several checkpoints in my day, to ask whether my spirit is that of one whose best friend has just been raised to life. In the various background moments of my day, I can keep telling myself, "The tomb is empty," or "Jesus is alive forever," or "I will not give my peace away," or "I want to live my life in this world, with my heart set on the world that will never end, with Jesus." As I encounter those situations of sin or darkness or death itself, which I looked at last week, I now let them be fully bathed in the light of Jesus' resurrection. If I'm faithful to this pattern each day, I should be able to recognize results in people's saying to me, "You seem different today—lighter, happier, freer somehow." By praying in everyday life this way, the worries don't disappear; rather, I can rely on a faith that frees me from their devastating effects on my spirit.

Each night I will find a brief moment to bring the day together in gratitude. When the morning grace I desire and some concrete event in my day's busyness come together, I need to recognize that as gift and give thanks. This ritual each evening increases my expectation the following day to find the joy of the Resurrection there.

Make use of the various resources provided for this week: the "For the Journey," "Scripture Readings," and sample words for our attempts at expression, in "In These or Similar Words . . ."

I may have begun this week with a low-grade sense of dis-courage-ment—"I don't know where they've taken him." By God's grace, I can end this week with a felt joy in the experience of Jesus alive, and a new courage as he says to me, "I am with you always."

For the Journey: The Garden of Resurrection

We pray this week with the joy of promises kept. Ignatius invites those who have made decisions to follow Christ to experience the grace of Christ's resurrection. We have considered the consequences of being faithful to being his companions. We have heard him telling the early companions that the world will hate them as it hates him. We have been invited to be in the world but not of it. He has prayed that we not be taken from the world but be a blessing within and about the world.

Mary, who stood at the foot of the cross, is the first to have promises kept to her. Ignatius piously pictures Jesus as appearing to his mother first after being raised from his tomb. As we earlier watched her fretfully consider the visit of the angel of the Annunciation, we now watch a most intimate embrace of mother and Son. As we watched and listened to Mary and Joseph's finding Jesus in the temple, we now joyfully watch and listen to Jesus finding Mary in her grief. We stood with Mary as they took Jesus down from the cross and laid him in a tomb; we gratefully consider Jesus comforting his faithful mother and companions as she experiences her own resurrection in that of her Son.

We may stay with that prayer view a long time and consider how Jesus has been released from his tomb to untomb us; as he has comforted his mother, he desires to comfort us.

There stood with Mary at the cross Mary Magdalene. In John's account of Jesus' rising, he first appears to this other woman of faith. It takes place in a garden and she supposes he is the gardener. So we visit the third garden of salvation. The garden of disobedience, where creation refused to listen; the garden of obedience, where the second Adam struggled and was faithful. Now we meet in the garden of resurrection.

The Gardener begins his graceful tending to the vines he has planted. He gently cultivates his branches after having pruned them all. Ignatius would have us be there and hear the Gardener mention our names, as he does here, "Mary." We are watching intimacy at work, comforting, raising up other bodies and spirits. We want to linger here watching the Gardener embrace his world.

In this scene, as with all the other contemplations during these weeks of the Resurrection, we see Jesus, because he is the Christ, urging whomever he meets back to, or out to, his mission of tending the garden. "Do not cling to me, but go . . ." Always intimacy moves to fruitfulness. The joy of his resurrection is that the love of God is not confined to a tomb but intensified in the lives of his found ones. The Humpty-Dumpty world is beginning to be put back together again by the risen Christ and his risen followers.

In These or Similar Words . . .

Dear Jesus,

Can it be real? Is this really you standing here in front of me? I watched from the foot of the cross as you suffered so incredibly and now, here you are in the garden, calling my name! Yes, Jesus, I am here with you! You are here! You are alive!

We hug and laugh and say nothing intelligible—just sounds of joy and awe. You are alive! I stop for a minute, thinking I am dreaming, but then I look into your eyes. Oh, my dear, dear friend, you have been raised from the dead. I will have you in my life!

There was such a loss when I saw you die but now, standing in this garden, you put your hands on my shoulder and look into my eyes again. We will not be apart anymore. "I will be with you always," you say to me and from deep in my heart, I can feel it.

Yes, you will be with me. I will stay with you. Together, Jesus, we will always be together! You are alive. You are here and then you hug me so gently and tell me you will see me later. There is no pang as you leave, no fear that you will not return. I feel your life so deeply within me in an odd, vivid way. It's joy and energy and a whole new way of being, of living, and of seeing the world. You are alive, my Jesus! Thank you for being in my life in such a deep way. Thank you for *being* my life.

Scripture Readings

Matthew 28:1–20
Luke 24:1–12
John 20:1–29

[Jesus] took some bread.
He blessed it and broke it.
Then he gave it to them.
At once they knew who he was.

—Luke 24:30–31

Jesus Is with Us

Guide: Recognizing Who He Is

The mystery of our everyday lives is that Jesus is with us, but we often don't recognize him. This week we will reflect on his presence with us, as we continue to ask for the grace of *joy with Jesus risen.*

When Jesus appeared to two disciples on the road to Emmaus, after his resurrection, they didn't know he was with them. They were quite caught up in their discouragement. Good Friday had been devastating to the hopes they had. They were so down because their expectations had died on that Friday. And in their self-pity, there was no room in their imagination for the Good News that God was trying to reveal to them.

This week we want to enter into the scene of the road to Emmaus and recognize this pattern in our lives. We will try to notice, through our background reflections each day, the ways we get absorbed in problems, discouragements, and worries and are unable to see Jesus with us.

We want to focus on two key parts of the story. Jesus makes the breakthrough in two ways.

He begins by "opening up the Scriptures to them." This is very much what Jesus has been doing for us during this retreat. We have come to understand the story and to appreciate how he came to enter our lives completely. We now know the patterns we face of not wanting to embrace our lives completely, resisting our own diminishment and death. The temptations to riches, honors, and pride abound. Jesus has been confronting our discouragement by revealing himself to us and inviting us to fall in love with him and his pattern of giving his life away. And we have seen the scandal of the cross as his revelation that his gift of self is for me. How often our hearts have burned within us!

Jesus then comes into their home with them and ritually gives them a way to recognize him and remember him. When he "took the bread," they must have seen him as the one who is there to nourish them with the daily bread that he promised would sustain them. When he "blessed it," they must have remembered how he gave thanks to God and placed his life in God's hands. When he "broke it," they knew he was the one whose life is broken open to reveal servant love to us. And, finally, when he "gave it to them," they knew who *they* were again—his disciples. Isn't this how we come to recognize him today?

Use the resources here to get started with this week. Our joy with Jesus grows this week as we come to know, through his self-revelation, in the way he gives himself to us in the breaking of bread, that he is alive and with us.

Some Practical Help for Getting Started This Week

We use the same practical way of proceeding in this week as we have throughout the retreat.

The Mystery We Contemplate

Here it is *Jesus alive and present with us*, even when in our discouragements, we fail to recognize him.

The Grace We Ask For

Here again we desire a deepening sense of *joy with Jesus*. For most of us, it is often easier to feel sorrow than joy, particularly the joy of another. All week long we want to find a way to ask God for the gift to enter more deeply in a joy for Jesus, risen and alive forever.

Our Daily Life Contemplation

This week we want to imagine the scene of Jesus walking along the road to Emmaus with those two distraught disciples. I want to get into that scene as much as possible. To identify with their saying "we had different hopes." To recall the story of salvation and the meaning of Jesus' life, which we have contemplated during this retreat. To share the experience of *recognition* in the breaking of bread.

The Daily Means

Each morning, among the first things I do is pause to focus on the grace I desire this week. As I put on my slippers or robe, I will pause for just a moment each morning and recall the *dynamic* I wish to be so conscious of this day: I can go through my day *without* a sense of Jesus' presence with me and it's in the *brokenness moments* that recognition can happen.

Throughout the day, in all the *background* times, I will return to these thoughts. This will help me be more conscious of Jesus' being with me. It will also help me see and experience the discouragements and really dark moments in my day in a very different way. Some examples might help.

I find myself at a meeting with several difficult people (or on the phone listening to a friend talk about a family conflict, or I'm watching television and seeing the terrible news of war or some violent crime). The moment I feel my spirit start to go down—in the presence of such conflicts or failures at reconciliation or outright evil—I will do a very brief exercise. *I will imagine Jesus: taking, blessing, breaking, and giving bread.* In that moment, I can be open to the grace of seeing that he is present here, in this situation, being broken and given, if only I open my eyes and see.

I find myself discouraged and beginning to get self-absorbed. (Each of us knows, by this point in the retreat, the situations that occasion this movement.) I will do this very brief exercise, acting against that movement. *I will imagine Jesus: taking, blessing, breaking, and giving me bread.* In that moment, I will no longer be alone. I will be opened to experience love and freedom. God's victory over this encounter with sin and death becomes very real. In this breaking-of-bread moment, in my everyday life, I recognize he is there. I feel the joy and I feel the freedom this joy gives.

Each night I will find a brief moment to bring the day together in gratitude. I will remember those times during the day when I felt his presence. I simply express my gratitude. I can feel the peace of those moments preparing my spirit to sleep more peacefully. Going to bed this way each night can make a tremendous difference in our lives.

Make use of the various resources provided for this week: the "For the Journey," and sample words for our attempts at expression, and "In These or Similar Words . . ."

As the *breaking-of-bread* moments of my week grow, they can form a fabric of *presence* moments that not only lift my spirit but also offer the gift of *abiding presence* that the Spirit of Jesus desires for us all, for God's greater glory and the service of others.

For the Journey: Companions

We turn to Luke's Gospel for his unique resurrection story. Two of Jesus' followers, who failed to see him in the breaking up of their personal hopes and failed to see him in the breaking up of his companions, will now recognize him "in the breaking of the bread."

As a "companion," or literally "with bread," is how Jesus comes alongside these two dispirited disciples. Their heads are down and they see the earth without any hope for the new life they had sought in the teachings of Jesus. As a companion he joins their darkness and gently leads them through their reflections on what has recently happened in Jerusalem. Their eyes are dimmer than their spirits, and they find it hard to believe what they saw happen and what they have heard about his resurrection. They didn't see it happen, so for them, it didn't really occur.

We watch and listen to their sharing in the rising of Jesus as their hearts burn within them while they listen to this mysterious companion. He is a collector, a finder, and he has risen to raise both those who seek for him and those who take the road back to Emmaus.

We find comfort and great joy in watching Jesus compassionately go out after those who have their hearts and hopes broken. It is so human to doubt and want to turn toward wherever our Emmaus hiding place may be. They freely turned to their own tombs burying their frustrated plans and fractured friendships. Our self-chosen tombs can be such comfortable resting places. These men are going back, and in meeting Jesus they will want not to go back, but to return.

We have been praying often these past weeks about our own tombs and hiding places. Their walls of fear, the locked doors of self-negativity and regret, have been abandoned, and yet we know their comforts and the easily found roads back to their ever-opened portals. It is very dark in our tombs and Jesus constantly invites us into the sunshine. The word *consolation* literally means "with the sunshine," and conversely *desolation* means "down out of the sunshine."

The men we watch these days experience the warmth of the sun in their being invited out of their darkness. The eucharistic "bread-withing" re-members them and they want to rejoin their companions, who themselves have been called out.

We pray this week with the joys of having been found, having been called out into the sunshine. We also pray with the joy in the awareness that he will always be collecting his followers in the breaking up of their hearts and hopes. He has risen so that we might have confidence in his grace more than our fragile selves. Easter is forever.

In These or Similar Words

Dear Jesus,

I read the story of the men on the road to Emmaus. I shake my head and wonder, How could they see you, someone they love and trust so much, and then not even recognize you? I would certainly recognize you . . . wouldn't I?

I feel like we've been through so much together. How could I not see you? Well, except maybe when I'm worried about how successful I am or how I look to others. Or wondering why I have to speak up about injustices to the poor when I am so busy already. I know I fail to be my best self so often, and I know how often you are there in that failure to forgive and support.

And now you are with me breaking bread, giving me not only this powerful way to remember you but to remind you of who I am with you. I am your disciple, walking along the road, often too distracted to see and sometimes walking the wrong direction and then you remind me about what I really need to know. You come disguised as my kids, or a dear friend, or an annoying neighbor. In each one of them, you are there, only sometimes you are harder to see.

But today, now, in this moment, I know you are with me and I rejoice! I know that even when I forget or can't see clearly, you are there in my heart, guiding, supporting, and loving me. And when I get past the confusion, I feel that passion for you in my heart. As I talked to you on the road to

Emmaus, my heart wasn't just warm, Jesus. It was burning inside. I feel different with you; I feel on fire with love for you. My life is so different with you in it, with such a close relationship with you, and I don't want to let it go.

So I forgive myself as I know you forgive me over and over for the times when I may not recognize you or the times I get so caught up in my own cares that I hurt or ignore someone else. Help me to recognize you in everyone around me.

Thank you, Lord, for the gift of Jesus in my life. Thank you for the joy I feel, the happiness of having Jesus in my life in this new, deeper, and stronger way. I truly feel the joy of Easter inside me, burning in my heart!

Scripture Readings

Luke 24:13–35

"Friends, have you caught anything?"
"No!'" they answered.
The net was so full of fish
    that they could not drag it up into the boat.
"Simon son of John, do you love me?"
    Peter was hurt because Jesus had asked him
    three times if he loved him. So he told Jesus,
"Lord, you know everything. You know I love you."
Jesus replied, "Feed my sheep."
Then he said to Peter, "Follow me!"

—John 21:5, 6, 17, 19

Jesus Is with Us— To Nourish Us for Our Mission

Guide: Feed My Sheep

Our final scene we contemplate in the Gospels prepares us for the end of this retreat. It's after the Resurrection. Peter says, "I'm going fishing." He doesn't know what to do with the resurrection of Jesus. Each of us could end this retreat and say, "I'm going back to whatever I was before."

This is a scene of re-calling. When Jesus asks them if they have caught anything, and then shows them their ability to haul in an enormous catch, with his power, they recognize him, as they hear their call again. This week, we can let our experiences of prayer—even in the background times—renew the call we have received in this retreat. The Lord, who is alive and with us in our everyday lives after this retreat, is the same Lord who has shown us such power in our lives these past months.

He is there with them—preparing food for them but inviting them to bring what they have received through his power. Haven't we experienced in this retreat that his nourishing presence is most effective when we have accepted his invitation to bring what we have been receiving to the table? Haven't we discovered that it's all gift, but that it is not received by passive waiting? Hasn't it taken some work and discipline on our part to bring previous gifts to the experience, in order to receive even more?

Jesus asks Peter about the degree of his love? How much? We see that the one who denied him three times is able to say that his love is three times stronger for that. And Jesus is then able to make the connection to mission—if you love *me*, then be *with me* in feeding my sheep. Aren't these the movements we have experienced in this retreat? Now, our joy with Jesus becomes fruitful. We are sent by the love we have for him. Having grown in love for him, we have grown in love for his mission.

Use the resources this week to enter more deeply into this week. Throughout the week, the dynamics of this scene can fill our consciousness with joy, gratitude, and growing freedom to give ourselves to nourish others.

Some Practical Help for Getting Started This Week

Our way of proceeding for this week takes us more deeply into the scene depicted in John 21.

The Mystery We Contemplate

This week we reflect on *Jesus alive and present with us as one who nourishes us for our mission.* Our reflection is in the context of our nearing the end of this retreat—as we look back and look forward.

The Grace We Ask For

We still seek a deepening sense of *joy with Jesus.* Jesus is risen and alive forever. We want to experience his presence, especially as we return to our daily life after this retreat. This week we desire to experience his renewing our call to be *with him* in his mission.

Our Daily Life Contemplation

This week we want to imagine that lakeside scene and its parts:

- Peter returns to fishing.

  I could end this retreat, saying "I'm returning to . . ."

- Jesus again shows them his power—a renewal of their call.

  *I have known his power these months, and his call,
  and long for its renewal now.*

- Jesus makes them breakfast and invites them to bring
  what they had already received.

  *I've experienced his feeding me and inviting me to
  actively bring what he's given me previously to that
  new experience of nourishment.*

- Jesus transforms Peter's three denials into three mis-
  sions to feed his people.

  *I know I'm a loved sinner, that I've grown in love for
  him and for his mission.*

- Jesus says to Peter, "Follow me."

  I hear that call and desire to say "yes."

The Daily Means

Each morning, among the first things I do is pause for just a
moment to focus on the grace I desire this week. As I put on
my slippers or robe, I will recall the *dynamic* I wish to be so
conscious of this day: my everyday life events are part of this
mystery. I'm nearing the end of this wonderful retreat experience. I have experienced the Lord's movements within me in
these daily moments these past months. Now I am renewed
in them and feel the call to be more deeply with Jesus in
his mission.

Throughout the day, in all the *background* times, I will
return to these thoughts. This will help me be more conscious
of Jesus' being with me. It will also help me see and experience
the graces I desire this week. Some examples might help.

Are there moments in my day when I experience *old patterns*, or *moments* within me that *return* to patterns that had been touched by grace in this retreat but now are still not what I desire? I want to be conscious of those times all week long. That is precisely where I can experience Jesus renewing his call and reminding me of his presence with me.

I might find myself *on the edge* of a grace experience. I've come to recognize it in this retreat before. There's a conflict or a struggle or some opportunity to surrender myself and help someone. I stop for a brief moment and see Jesus there, making me breakfast. And he says, so calmly and with such confidence in my companionship with him, "Bring to this experience some of what I've allowed you to receive. This moment can be nourishment, if you bring to it what I've given you."

There are lots of choice moments in our week. Am I going to do something this way or that way? Am I going to go to this or go to that? Will I try to save my life or lose it in loving others? At those choice crossroads, I can pause briefly and listen to Jesus ask, "Do you love me?" I can let the words and feelings be expressed, "Yes, Lord, you know that I love you." In that concrete life moment, I will let Jesus say, "Then choose what will be an act of nourishment for others."

Throughout my day, as I walk from one place to another, or get in the car to go to my next commitment, I can hear Jesus' call, "Follow me." And in that background moment, I breathe a peaceful "Yes, Lord, I am with you, here."

Each night I will find a brief moment to bring the day together in gratitude. Expressing my thanks each evening will help me grow in confidence that Jesus is indeed present, nourishing me this day for mission with him.

Make use of the various resources provided for this week: the "For the Journey" and sample words for our attempts at expression in "In These or Similar Words . . ."

As the "yes" moments of my week grow, they can form a fabric of nourishing mission moments that not only lift my spirit but also offer the gift of companionship in mission with Jesus that his Spirit desires for us all, for God's greater glory and the service of others.

For the Journey: Come Follow Me

Simon Peter is about to be caught again by the Fisherman. Again we watch and listen to all that is going on.

It is daybreak; it is no longer night. Jesus as light has come to illumine the dark and "overcome the darkness." Peter had denied his teacher three times while warming himself at night by a charcoal fire.

Perhaps Jesus has a loving smile as he prepares a charcoal fire around which he will initiate a reconciliation with his student. The scene is set. Where are you sitting or standing? Perhaps you can stand next to Jesus as he again invites his friends to face the fact: not that they aren't good fishermen but to remember his words, "Apart from Me you can do nothing." So he asks them if they have caught anything. Their brief negative answer heightens the drama.

Perhaps Jesus asks you whether it is time for the big catch. They are the ones who will be caught by following the instructions of Jesus. They make a great haul and so does Jesus. Peter gets a funny feeling that he has seen this picture before, and he jumps into the water and makes his way into the light of the morning. There is the fish already cooking and Jesus gently invites Peter to bring some of the other fish for a fine breakfast. Jesus offers them bread and fish as a sign that it is really him; he has come to catch them up in his net of forgiveness.

This is not the happy ending though. As you sit with them, Peter needs something more than breakfast; he needs some words, some conversation, to make this all real. So Jesus, knowing this human need in us all, directly asks Peter three times, while warming himself again by a charcoal fire, "Do you love me?" Three times Peter unties the knot of denial with which he bound himself in the darkness. Jesus is not insisting, He is loosening and freeing Peter from his shame. This is still not the happy ending.

The happy ending has echoes of the first happy beginning when Jesus first called Peter to "be not afraid" and "come follow me." Jesus reminds Peter of his first call and his first beginning. Peter looks back to where he has been and then forward to the unknown where of his future. "When you were young you put on your own belt and walked where you liked, but when you grow old, you will stretch out your hands, and someone else will put a belt round you and take you where you would rather not go."

This is the happy ending, though it might sound somber and frightening. Peter follows Jesus, though he does have some concerns about his friend John: "What about him?"

We are called this week to again be caught by his love. Again we are asked to put our regrets and infidelities into the charcoal fire. Again we have our own questions about our futures, but he calls us again back to our dignity as his sisters and brothers. We would like to stay on the shore eating bread and fish. We would like to build three tents here and not hand out any maps. We have prayed enough these weeks to know that He was sent to us, "as the Father has sent me, so I send you." Reconciliation, nourishing, gathering, comforting, are all essential elements of being on mission with Christ.

So we pick up the pieces of bread and fish and they go with us as signs that he came to stay while being with us as men and women for others.

In These or Similar Words . . .

Dear Jesus,

What a joy to be here on the beach with you! After the drama and excitement of the past weeks, it was nice to get away from it all, to go back to what I know, my simple life—the life I led before I met you.

But then as I sat in the boat with Peter and the others, idling in the last moments of a long night, catching nothing, we saw you calling to us from the shore. Peter plunged into the water and swam in, while the rest of us laughed and got the boat into shore as quickly as we could. It's you! I am so thrilled to be here with you.

Did I really think my life would ever return to "normal"? What was I thinking? What in the world is normal to me now? I'm sitting here with you, my beloved friend, as you make me breakfast and ask how I am. Yes, I've been a little overwhelmed by the events of recent weeks as I tried to stay with you through it all. I've been so joyful that you are back and are with me at such a deep level. But what does that mean for my life, Jesus?

What will happen to me now? How will this joy I feel in you and for you affect my life? You ask if I care for you. *Yes!* Yes, dearest friend, I care for you and love you so much. I will feed your sheep. I will tend to your flock, to the poor and the downtrodden, as you have. Is that what you are asking of me? Is that how I can continue to feel you in my life—to care for your sheep?

And then you looked so deeply into my eyes, with such love and understanding and said, "Follow me." I will! Yes, I will follow you! Maybe I held back a little on the boat, afraid of taking the plunge into the water as Peter did, but no longer. I am ready to follow you, to feed your sheep. Show me where, tell me how!

Thank you, Jesus, for such joy! My heart is soaring with love for you. Thank you for holding my hand past the fears of the unknown and asking me to follow you. I'm not sure what my "yes" is or where it will take me, but *yes!*

Scripture Readings

John 21:1–19

Take, Lord, and receive all my liberty,
my memory, my understanding,
and my entire will,
all that I have and possess.
Thou hast given all to me.
To Thee, O Lord, I return it.
All is Thine, dispose of it wholly
according to Thy will.
Give me Thy love and Thy grace,
for this is sufficient for me.

—*The Spiritual Exercises of St. Ignatius*,
No. 234

God's Love for Us, Our Response

Guide: Gratitude

Let us reflect on God's love for us and our response.

Next week is the final week of retreat. This week we look back, to contemplate what we have received in this retreat—*God's love itself.* And we consider *our response.* Our desire for this week is *to be filled with a deep sense of the gifts we have received,* and so filled with profound gratitude, we will be moved *to love and serve God, in all things,* in our everyday lives. Two convictions guide our reflections:

- Love expresses itself in deeds rather than mere words.

  Love is the gift of self for the other.

- Love that is reciprocal grows.

  Lovers give of themselves to each other, with each deep gift leading to a deeper response.

This week we will recall all of the gifts of love we have received during this retreat. We will remember all the ways God has given us graces that were the gift of self. We want to grow in gratitude for the activity of God's love for us, especially in the gift of Jesus for us, and the ways in which we have been blessed to know, love, and serve with Jesus.

This week we want to open our hearts to the broadest sense of God's love that we can imagine. Using images like the rays of the sun's warm light or the overwhelming power of a constant waterfall, we will consider how God's life-giving presence and love flow in and through all of creation, given to and for us.

Use the resources this week to enter into these exercises of appreciation in detail.

With each level of gratitude, we want to express our love. Our response, and our offering of self in love, is what seals and strengthens the bonds of love between us and God. We will grow in a sense that all we have is gift. As we have grown in freedom, we can surrender ourselves in love more and more completely.

All week, with growing gratitude and deepening affection, I will make offerings of myself in these or similar words, until they become mine:

> *Take, Lord, and receive*
> *all my liberty, my memory,*
> *my understanding, my entire will—*
> *all that I am and possess.*
> *You have given all this to me.*
> *I now return it all to you.*
> *It is yours now.*
> *Use these gifts according to your will.*
> *Give me only your love and your grace.*
> *That is enough for me, and all that I desire.*

Some Practical Help
for Getting Started This Week

Our contemplation on the love of God for us, and our response, can be done both in several prayer periods and in the background times throughout our week.

What We Are Considering

For all these months, we have considered our relationship with God. We now draw it all together to understand and appreciate all that God has given us in this retreat, in our lives, and what God continues to give us.

- The blessings of creation, redemption, and the special graces I have received.

- God dwelling in every part of creation, especially in me.

- How God labors for me in all of creation, giving and sustaining life.

- How all blessings and gifts descend—as the sun's light and water flowing from a fountain.

And we will consider our response.

The Grace We Ask For

Our desire for this week is to be filled with a deep sense of the gifts we have received, and so filled with profound gratitude, we will be moved to love and serve God, in all things, in our everyday lives. The prayer for this week helps us ask for this grace.

Our Daily Life Contemplation

It is very important to try to focus our attention this week on gratitude for God's love. The two convictions about love from our guide are critical: love consists more in deeds than in words, and love involves the mutual exchange of gifts between lovers. It would be very helpful to set aside some brief prayer times, using this simple help:

- Begin by feeling the presence of God.

- Ask for the grace I desire—an intimate sense of God's love for me.

- Reflect on God's love:
  - What has God done for me?
  - What has God given me?
  - How does God sustain me?
  - What is God offering me?

- Speak, lover to lover, with words, feelings of gratitude.

- Write down what I wish to remember.

These are not just intellectual reflections. We are asking for intimacy here, and our goal is that our memory and our accounting of God's gifts will fill us with deep and moving gratitude and stir our hearts to a response of love and service.

The Daily Means

These reflections will become a part of the movements of our everyday lives this week if we can make use of the means we've been practicing for so long. It involves how we *focus* at the beginning and end of each day. If we get up each day and capture a moment to focus our consciousness and desire for the day, at the time we do something very routine (like putting on our slippers or robe), we develop a pattern that will serve us very well this week and all our lives. It changes the way we experience our busy days. That brief moment is *there* every morning. We just need to use it. And if we take a similar moment each night, before we go to bed, at a routine time, we can end each day receiving and giving thanks for the graces we receive. In that brief, nightly moment we can grow in awareness of God's activity in our busy days and become more and more grateful, even in the most difficult of times.

There are opportunities throughout the day, in all the *background* times we have. Driving, walking from one place to another, pausing to think, transitioning from one thing to another. Those times are *there*, no matter how brief. They are usually filled with something—some worry or planning or daydreaming. We can use them—even if they are thirty seconds long—to focus our attention, to return to the thought and desire of the morning, to note how *this upcoming event of my day* fits into this desire I have. Some examples might help.

I am taking a shower. My mind is already zooming about the day ahead. Can I focus, for just a minute, for even a simple prayer? "Lord, help me to know you are with me today. I need you. Help me to stay open to discover ways you love me."

I am driving to work. My mind is perhaps filled with what I need to do today. Perhaps I have others in the car with me. Perhaps it's my habit to listen to the radio. Can I take just a moment to return my focus to the Lord's presence? It will change how I listen to the radio or deal with the people I'm with in the car. Perhaps I am alone and can turn the radio off and give myself twenty or thirty minutes of time to focus and reflect. I could look at each of the events in my upcoming day and prepare to enter into them in the way I desire.

There will inevitably be some challenges in my day, perhaps even some conflicts. As I become more and more reflective, I will become more and more familiar with the patterns I display. In the approach to those situations and people, I can take just a moment and let the *background* reflection prepare me. Perhaps I can take a slow, deep breath and in fifteen seconds pray: "Lord, I know you love me. Let me experience your sustaining love and care here." Or "Lord, you have forgiven me so many times for this pattern. Thank you for your love and mercy. Fill me with your peace now." Or "Lord, you have let me desire to be *with you* before. Let me be *with you* here, so that your love can flow through me." Or "Take, Lord, receive.

I offer myself to you in this. Give me only your love and your grace. I ask for nothing more."

Whether I find time for prayer periods this week or do my reflections throughout the week in the background times, it can be very profitable to keep repeating the "Take, Lord, receive" prayer. Perhaps I can memorize it or find my own words for it.

Make use of the various resources provided for this week, especially "For the Journey" and the sample words for prayer in "In These or Similar Words . . ."

The whole retreat comes together this week. The Lord who brought us along this path will continue to bless us with his love and with the grace for our response.

For the Journey: Marvels

This final exercise of the retreat is modeled on the final reflection in the Spiritual Exercises. There is an irony here. Though it is the final exercise, the making of the Exercises never ends. God does not send us a certificate proclaiming, "You have successfully finished the course." Paul himself wrote that he had not reached the finish line but pressed on. So we finish our beginning and continue our being created and re-created by the love of God. Two points for Ignatius were very important during these last exercises: love consists more in deeds than in words, and love is a mutual handing over to the other of all that one has. In the first "For the Journey" we are encouraged not to look for progress or lack of it during our journeys. Instead, we have been encouraged to watch Love at work, manifesting that love in deeds and in the handing over to us all the gifts of grace and life that we have been offered.

This week we pray with the receptivity of children who sense how deeply they are loved. Ignatius wrote the Exercises to be very personal and so we move from the general *we* to the very particular *I*.

There are the children in our culture, who at the end of opening all their Christmas presents might have a feeling of "Is this all there is?" Maybe after evaluating his or her siblings' gifts, he or she might feel cheated or less loved. This is very human and understandable.

I am encouraged to be the Christmas-presented child who, after seeing my gifts and those of others, wants to look at my parents and relatives and wonder, "Why are they so good and loving to me?"

It is in this spirit of grateful wonder that Ignatius asks me to make some response of love freely. "All I have, You have given me. What I can give You back is my selfish, possessive and exclusive possession and use of them. I ask only that You bless and grace me in our future together. That would be enough for me and a beginning for You."

I walk through a world of created gifts. Trees, flowers, birds of all sizes and kinds, amazingly diverse, and all these presents given to me.

I look up at the moon, the stars, I marvel at the changes of the weather as the sun moves back and forth keeping this world at the proper temperatures for life and growth. All this God hands over to me.

I return to the childlike puzzling at the littlest things and muse that God has always and is always at work to hand things to me. God is laboring to attract me but not force me to see the divine finger and hand and arm and self, creating me and all else for me as well. This exercise increases my awareness of how everything is a gift and at the same time an invitation. I am both the recipient and the responder. Once I am aware of how God exists in everything and everything exists in God, how can I keep from singing, from watching and listening, from sharing and from wanting to know what is being offered at any one moment of my life? The river of God's love flows on whether or not I am attentive to its presents and presence. I want to be less unavailable to the Giver of Love who works and does things in my life so as to reduce me to the wondering child of God I am. The "child of God" is a mature human who knows what things are, where they have come from, and where they are taking me. All things that come from God return to God, including me.

We leave this retreat to live so that we constantly recover sight and sensitivity to the goodness of God and the goodness of this God-love self who I am.

In These or Similar Words . . .

Dearest friend Jesus,

My heart is so full. I feel loved and honored and graced and flawed and loved all over again. I am full of wonder for the love I feel from you and for you. Yes, I am so aware of my flaws and how they sometimes keep me from feeling the love you are pouring on me at every moment. But right now I also feel your deep love and care for me, especially right there, in my weaknesses, those parts of me I want to hide in the dark. Your love brings it out into the light of your warmth and suddenly, I seem to be freer from it.

Now, after these many months of talking with you, loving you, and accepting your love in a whole new way, I realize that you will always, always be with me, even in—or especially in—my weaknesses.

And the gifts! So many gifts you have lavished on me over my lifetime. I feel so deeply your love for me. I see the many ways you love me each day, in the world around me, in the many people you put into my life to love me each day.

The line from Scripture returns to me over and over as I ponder this joyful puzzle: What return can I make for all that the Lord has given me? What is it, Jesus? How can I ever show you the kind of love I feel for you or thank you for all you have given me? I want to give you everything I have.

I want to respond to these many gifts in some way that comes from the deepest part of my being, and every time I think of the many ways you have loved me and given me gifts, I know I want to give you everything I have.

Jesus, you have given me so much, just as the prayer says: my mind, my liberty, memory, understanding, my entire will, and my being. Everything I am in this life, I am because of what you have given me. What can I ever do to thank you? Please, dear friend, may I present these gifts back to you? Can I ask you to use them in this world, for your world, in any way you would like? I want to be free enough to offer you my life. What would you like to do with it? How can I use my life to serve you in this world? How can I love others, as you would like me to?

I look forward with great joy to the weeks and months ahead, dear Jesus, so that together, as we continue to talk, I will discover the answers to these questions.

I thank you for my life. I thank you with my life.

God is the one who began this good work in you,
and I am certain that he won't stop before it is
complete on the day that Christ Jesus returns.

We must keep going in the direction that we
are now headed.

—Philippians 1:6, 3:16

Let Us Reflect
on the Path before Us

Guide: Contemplatives in Action

This retreat is ending in one sense. In another, it will continue in the way it has changed our lives.

Unlike a retreat to a retreat house, we didn't retreat from our everyday lives. The path before us will be shaped by what new patterns we have developed through these exercises. During this final week, we want to identify the patterns we desire and choose the path before us.

The "Prayer to Begin Each Day" gives a sense of our ongoing prayer:

May all that I am today, all that I try to do today, may all my encounters, reflections, even the frustrations and failings, all place my life in your hands. Lord, my life is in your hands. Please, let this day give you praise.

The grace we ask for this week is simple: that our Lord would *guide us in choosing how we will live our lives more with and in Jesus.*

We owe the inspiration for this retreat to Ignatius of Loyola, the founder of the Society of Jesus (the Jesuits) and the author of the *Spiritual Exercises.* He has been our guide in recognizing God's invitation to freedom; God's mercy; God's plan to save us; God's invitation that we join Jesus in his mission; and God's grace in allowing us to come to know, love, and desire to serve with Jesus most intimately. After guiding people through the Exercises, Ignatius would sometimes receive letters complaining that it was difficult to be contemplative in the midst of a busy life. He would always answer that it was more important to be *contemplatives in the midst of action.* He explained that for those who had found intimacy with God in prayer, it would be *easy to find intimacy with God in all things.* He always included one qualifying addition: *if* they continued to *die to self-love* and *act against* whatever tempted them away from freedom to love of others.

As we go through each day this week, let us ask:

- How do I want to keep naming my desires before God?

- How can I keep focused, in the background times?

- What patterns do I choose to make a habit?

- Which ones will I choose to be free from?

- Who, and in what ways, will I love as I have been loved?

- What will "dying to self-love" mean for me?

- What choices does living with and in Jesus lead me to?
  - About my current and future life goals?
  - About my lifestyle?

- About my relationships?
- About my solidarity with and concern and
  care for the poor?

The resources here offer concrete help for making this week a wonderful transition to everyday life.

Please consider making use of the prayer resources on the Creighton Online Ministries Web site.

Some Practical Help for Getting Started This Week

"Getting started" this week takes on another meaning. This week will be our transition to a daily life after the retreat. Our reflections will take us into our desires for the future and our choices about putting those desires into action.

What We Are Considering

We want to look back over this retreat and consider the patterns that were the means through which God's graces flowed into our hearts. We want to understand the path that brought us to where we are now, so that we can continue on it for the future. We want to resolve to live our lives as contemplatives in action, by finding intimacy with Jesus in all we do.

The Grace We Ask For

Our desire for this week is that our Lord would guide us in choosing how we will live our lives more **with** and **in** Jesus.

Our Daily Life Contemplation

Last week our gratitude for all God has done for us stirred our hearts to a response of love and service. If that kind of reflecting proved to be helpful, it would be very important to stay there and to continue growing in gratitude and to continue making the offering of self expressed by the prayer Take, Lord, Receive. We may want to keep finding ways to say that prayer, or our version of it, each day, at a specific time, in order to move it more deeply inside our consciousness.

This week we want to *name* what it is that we intend to make a part of our life after the retreat. We want this to be a creative part of the process in the continuing relationship God desires with us.

By this time in the retreat we have developed some habits. We want to *recognize* those and let God *show us* the path before us.

How We Began Our Day

- What did I do each morning to begin my day *focusing* on the grace I desired?

- Did I use a simple, daily routine, like putting on my slippers or robe, to fix this as a daily prayer moment?

- What do I choose to resolve to do from now on?

How We Ended Our Day

- What did I do each night to end my day, collecting my day, in gratitude?

- Did I use a simple, daily routine, like taking my clothes off or brushing my teeth, to fix this as a daily prayer moment?

- What do I choose to resolve to do from now on?

How We Used the *Background* Times in Our Day

- What did I do to carry on a conversation with my Lord throughout my day, if even for thirty-second periods?

- Did I use the brief spaces in my day, between things, to be contemplative in action?

- What do I choose to resolve to do from now on?

Other Patterns That Made This Retreat So Open to Grace

- Were there new ways I let these reflections into my everyday life?

- Did I experience the conflicts, difficult times, differently because of how I placed them in the context of being with and in Jesus during this retreat?

- What do I choose to resolve to do from now on?

Other Choices We Can Consider

One choice is to use the Daily Reflections and the Weekly Guide to Daily Prayer on the Creighton Online Ministries Web site for ongoing support for prayer in everyday life.

Some may feel themselves desiring to make a weekend or weeklong retreat at a retreat center. Making this choice can be a powerful gift one could give oneself to deepen the graces of the retreat. Locate a Jesuit retreat center to contact for more information.

For all of us, we will want to make choices about the *ways* we will *de-selfish* our living of our everyday lives. We will want to name concrete people and concrete situations where our *loving* will be expressed.

Some will want to choose to make some choices to become more involved in *service* for others, beyond our families and work situations, through our parish or congregation. Some means of getting to know and being in solidarity with those who are poor can be a most profound means of staying in touch with the movements of God in our hearts.

Sharing the graces of this retreat with others can be an important choice. It will not only ground us more deeply in the experience but also will let the grace be not only for us and maybe fruitful for someone else. Our consoling experience of the hundreds of e-mails we have received from around the world underlines the power of sharing.

Make use of the various resources provided for this week: especially "For the Journey" and the sample words for our attempts at expression in "In These or Similar Words . . ."

At the end of the Eucharist, the priest may use several dismissals. One of them seems very appropriate at the end of this retreat. "Let us go forth in peace, to love and serve the Lord." And the people respond, "Thanks be to God."

For the Journey: "I Was Blessed"

Graduation, which is the ending ceremony, is also called commencement. *Commence* means to begin, and so the graduates are celebrated as those beginning their new lives.

One might think that one makes the Spiritual Exercises in such a way that there ought to be an ending ceremony and a commencement or graduation. Baptism is our beginning and our resurrection is the eternal ongoing fulfillment of that life. It never ends, and so too with the exercise of our spirits. No person who has begun the Spiritual Exercises can say that they "have made" them. We have been concentrating on our beginnings and the work of the Holy Spirit never ends. The working of the Evil Spirit never ends. The workings of our own fallen selves never end.

We are similar to a garden whose weeds seem to multiply the more we pick them. Our spiritual weeds have always been there—"some enemy hath done this." What has been going on during this retreat is a process of becoming aware and not discouraged or negative about those weeds of which we have become aware.

We are commencing, then, to let God continue to attract us to the ways of Jesus. We will always have our own ways, which may dissect and contradict his ways. We have watched him walk our ways and have heard his call to insult the ways of this world and our cultures of violence, greed, and power. We have admitted that we live in a tension between God's call and the many other calls that are so attractive. We have prayed that God would take our gifts of liberty, memory, and will. We have become aware that we will slowly, and maybe not so slowly, want to find ways to take those gifts back. This is not a cause to be frustrated or feel hypocritical. We are loved by being created, loved by being called, loved in being saved, and loved by being on pilgrimage.

We are those who believe that keeping on keeping on, is what God loves us into doing. Will any graduate live what she or he hears during the graduation speeches or even all that he or she has learned? We walk off the stage of this retreat knowing we will return to find out where we have gone and to hear his call again to be the beloved of God.

> *My fiftieth year had come and gone;*
> *I sat a solitary man in a London shop,*
> *An open book and an empty chafe cup on a marble table top.*
> *While on the shop and street I gazed,*
> *Of a sudden my body blazed,*
> *And twenty minutes more or less,*
> *It seemed so great my happiness,*
> *That I was blessed and I could bless.*

—William Butler Yeats

In These or Similar Words . . .

Dearest friend Jesus,

I feel you with me now, close by my side, holding my hand as I begin the walk down the road. I'm not sure where it is leading, but I know that I am both following you and walking with you as we go.

Peacefulness has seeped into my soul and I feel like nothing can disturb me. Together we will walk through this world, through this life, and I will have the love and care that have changed my life. My life is different now than it was thirty-four weeks ago. In some ways I am very changed and in some ways I am so much the same.

It seems like what I do with my life will be different now. I know I will make choices that people won't understand, and I will face decisions that frighten me. Sometimes I will fall back on what I know best or what is easiest and will make the wrong choice. But I know I can turn to you, look into your eyes, and talk about it.

Help me, gentle Jesus, in my life as I try to live a life of self-giving, not considering my needs first but those of others. Give me the wisdom and courage to make the right choices, to have a faith that does justice and a life that always cares for the poor.

I know that I am not perfect and maybe—finally—I understand that is something to rejoice in. I can be happy in my imperfections and my weaknesses because it is there that you come to me so gently to support and love me.

I feel you with me at all times, in all that I do and in everyone I see. Give me the patience and insight to recognize you in the people who annoy or frighten me, the people I don't understand. Let me see your eyes looking back at me when I speak to them.

What I want the most, what I feel so very deeply, is that I want to live a life of service to you by serving others. I want to be where you want me to be and live as you want, without hearing the self-serving echoes of the world.

Please help me in my struggle to be free from anything that keeps me from loving and serving you. All I want in my life is to love you.

Thank you so much for all you are in my life. Please accept these tears in my eyes, the great love in my heart, and the life I to offer you. It is everything I have.

Give me only your love and your grace. I want nothing more.

Lent is a gift.
Open it up.

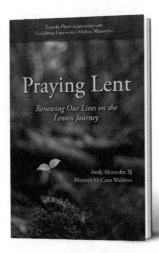

Praying Lent
Renewing Our Lives
on the Lenten Journey
ISBN-13:
978-0-8294-2857-5
5½" x 8½" • 88 pages
$5.95

Incorporating many principles of Ignatian spirituality, *Praying Lent* provides readers with a rich, full, and transformative Lenten experience. From how to realign our priorities to how to celebrate Lent in the home, from helping the poor to experiencing reconciliation and healing, this book opens up the purpose of Lent—it is a time for us to grow prayerfully, personally, and powerfully in our relationship with God.

This book, like *Retreat in the Real World*, is published by Loyola Press in partnership with Creighton University's Online Ministries.

Two online resources to help you nurture a lived faith!

The 3-Minute Retreat
www.loyolapress.com/retreat

Through inspiring photography, soothing music, and daily Scripture verses, the 3-Minute Retreat lets you take a short prayer break whenever you need it most. Simply log on to **www.loyolapress.com/retreat** to begin this peaceful prayer experience.

Creighton University's Online Ministries
www.Creighton.edu/CollaborativeMinistry/online.html

From daily reflections to audio retreats to seasonal prayers, this Web site offers numerous opportunities for you to find God in everyday life. Log on to **http://www.Creighton.edu/CollaborativeMinistry/ online.html** and discover new ways to grow in your faith amidst the busyness of life.